Haven't We Gone Through This Before?

Haven't We Gone Through This Before?

Breaking Out of Those Parent-Child Ruts

Richard L. Berry

Foreword by Vernon Grounds

Fleming H. Revell
A Division of Baker Book House Co
Grand Rapids, Michigan 49516

© 1996 by Richard L. Berry

Published by Fleming H. Revell
a division of Baker Book House Company
P.O. Box 6287, Grand Rapids, MI 49516-6287

Printed in the United States of America

Library of Congress Cataloging-in-Publication Data

Berry, Richard L., 1950–
    Haven't we gone through this before? : breaking out of those parent-child ruts / Richard L. Berry.
      p.   cm.
    ISBN 0-8007-5579-0 (pbk.)
    1. Parent and child. 2. Child rearing. I. Title.
HQ755.85.B479   1996
649'.1–dc20   95–44540

To
Beth and Jim Berry
Pat and Charlie Stoehrmann
for
providing a "good picture"
of what it means to parent

Contents

Contents

Foreword

Not another book on parenting! Isn't there already a plethora of publications, many of them helpful and Christianly oriented, which advise mothers and fathers on how to bring up children, solve discipline problems, and avoid emotional breakdown in the process? Yes, a super-abundance of such material is now available. But while I am grateful for all those resources, I must say that Dr. Richard Berry has given us a down-to-earth, understandable, and specific manual that will prove a godsend indeed to conflicted and troubled families.

Dr. Berry does not write as a theoretician, but as a practitioner with long, firsthand experience in counseling parents and children whose relationships have degenerated into ruts of impasse and mutual unhappiness. What he does, therefore, is first explain why and how ruts develop; then with humor and true-life examples, he outlines step-by-step procedures for breaking out of those ruts.

This is a *must* read for frustrated parents and for individuals—therapists, pastors, social workers—who are seeking to prevent rutted relationships from forming and to change those already formed into conjunctive patterns of family interaction.

Vernon Grounds
President Emeritus
Denver Seminary

Acknowledgments

Thanks to the many people who made valuable contributions to this manuscript. Without their assistance it wouldn't have been completed.

Bonnie Berry: Kept the family activities running while I sat at the computer. You are an inspiration of dedication and perseverance. Thanks for being an excellent co-parent–I have learned much from you.

My children–Mike, Brian, and Melissa: Provided a more than adequate testing ground for our parental skills and kept this manuscript focused on practical ways of getting the job done. Thanks for allowing me to share portions of our family life with others. I'm very proud of you.

Alona Scheer: Spent countless hours editing, correcting my grammar, and questioning if what I said was really what I meant. Without her excellent work and labor of love, the manuscript would never have been seriously considered for publication. You are a talented and gifted friend.

Sherry Goodman: Promoted the book and its content even before it was completed. She also provided much needed encouragement and prayer through some difficult waiting periods. Thanks for continuing to believe in the material.

Jan Bailey: Helped to create new directions through her ideas and humor. Your creativity is amazing.

David Downing: Provided needed direction for pursuing publication avenues in the world of Christian publishing. Your assistance, direction, and encouragement were very helpful.

Kathy Buteau and Ronn Jeffrey: Gave needed feedback for narrowing the scope of this manuscript. Thanks for being clear and direct.

Rebecca Bailly, Bobbie Blount, Rita Biggerstaff, and Bob Norris: Read and critiqued the manuscript at various stages and provided encouragement to continue.

Kerry Bailey, Dave Goodman, Sherry Welch: Provided encouraging words at just the right time.

Families at Youth Alternatives: Provided many different and difficult situations that confront parents who are trying to be good parents. Thanks for sharing your families, your struggles, and your successes.

Meadowbrooke Baptist Church: The church, particularly the adult Sunday school class, provided an opportunity to "test" the information in a group setting. Thanks for your support and encouragement.

Vernon Grounds: Helped begin the process of obtaining a publisher. Thanks for your continued support. Your faith is a personal inspiration to many.

Gwen Ellis: Provided valuable feedback on how to make the manuscript more appealing to the reader. Thanks for the personal touch.

Cathy and Lee Swanson: Suggested that I could write a book that would be useful for parents! I appreciated your idea, ongoing support, and pleasure in sharing in this process.

PART 1

Patterns

*If you do what you
have always done,
you will get
what you have
always gotten.*

1

Doing What
We've Always Done

How much actual training in parenthood have you had? In all likelihood, you have had more training in operating a gas barbecue grill.

Permit me to illustrate. With the purchase of your gas grill, you received an instruction manual that included the following:

1. Description of the model
2. List of needed tools
3. Leakage checklist
4. Operating instructions
5. Troubleshooting guide
6. Limited warranty
7. Toll-free number for help
8. Return policy

Wow! Wouldn't it be great to receive this kind of information with each new bundle of joy?

The model description helps you understand how one model differs from other models. Each of your children is unique, so it would be helpful to know how to deal with their differences.

The tool list could suggest items for the baby shower. Got a loose nut? Use the proper tool to fix it.

The leakage checklist might help you through the frustrations of potty training.

Operating instructions would assure you that if you followed certain steps, your kids would turn out a certain way.

Every mom and dad would welcome an accurate troubleshooting guide for malfunctioning adolescents.

The warranty would be a hot item. I frequently receive phone calls from concerned parents questioning their liability.

"What happens if my child runs away?"

"Who pays for the windows he broke in the neighbor's car?"

"Am I responsible for the charge my son made on my VISA for a new set of drums?"

The toll-free number for help would undoubtedly require round-the-clock staffing with many operators standing by.

The return policy could be a good safety valve. Though you'd probably never use it, on certain days there might be some comfort in knowing that it was an option.

Unfortunately these items don't come with babies. (What you can count on are many surprises, high expectations of what you *should* be able to do, and of course many bills.) If a gas grill came without the instruction manual we would be upset by the lack of support provided by the company. Yet when rearing children and managing a family, we think we should be able to do the job without training or assistance.

Okay, so making a family function smoothly isn't as easy as we anticipated, and joking about it won't fix it (although humor certainly lightens the strain). However, if we want to fix something, we must first determine what is wrong. With so much happening in a family, it's difficult to know where to look and what to change.

Let's begin to narrow the focus a bit with a personal incident.

It is 6:14 A.M. on a cold, dark Monday. The snooze alarm goes off for the third time, and I'm having a hard time getting out of my warm waterbed. A full schedule awaits me at work, so I really must get moving. I turn the alarm off again, take a deep breath, muster all of my determination, and fall back asleep. The next time I look at the clock it is ten minutes past the critical time. What a way to start a Monday.

I stumble into the bathroom. Over the noise of the shower, I hear my wife Bonnie say, "You'd better hurry! You always shower the same way. If you don't change that today, you'll be late."

Now what sort of comment is that to make to a half-asleep person who has a doctorate in psychology? I think to myself, "I shower the same way? I'm not sure that's true, but how would she know?" Life is starting to ooze back into my brain. I ask, "Dear, what do you mean I 'always shower the same way'?"

We all have unique patterns of behavior.

She quickly replies, "You always wash in the same way. First you stand under the shower and get your hair wet, then you get wet all over, then you wash under your arms . . ."

I poke my head out of the shower to see if she's standing there watching me, but she's in the next room. What's strange is that she is right. There are patterns to almost everything I do.

We all have patterns of behavior that are easily recognizable by those who know us well. We usually pay little attention to a pattern unless others point it out. Sometimes we agree with the observation and sometimes it surprises us.

Take a moment and review your day. What patterns can you see in your behavior? Like me, you probably showered the same way you always do. If you went to the grocery store to do the weekly shopping, you probably followed your usual path through the store. When you cleaned your house or changed the oil in your car, it's likely that you did it much the same way as last time. You probably drove to work via the same route. Your friends could have ordered your lunch with little difficulty. If you attended a meeting, your colleagues could have predicted whether you'd speak up, monopolize the conversation, or remain pensively silent.

Internal motivations consisting of our interests, preferences, goals, and beliefs cause us to act consistently over time, producing patterns of behavior.

Like individuals, families have identifiable and predictable behavior patterns.

You may readily agree that individuals have recognizable patterns, but you might not have applied this same concept to families. If you did, you would find that families also have identifiable patterns. This occurs because we blend our individual patterns of behavior together to produce consistent, identifiable parent-child interactions. Your response influences your child's response, which in turn influences your response, and so on. Over time, and through many cycles, a consistent pattern emerges. For both the parent and the child, each pattern consists of an underlying motivation that produces consistent behavior responses.

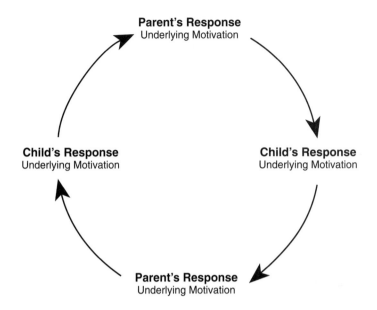

Let me illustrate: A teenage boy, Ryan, is asked to do a household chore but does only a marginal job. When his dad criticizes him, Ryan expends even less energy, thus producing a more inferior result.

At first we might fault Dad for being too critical. But if we talked to Dad about his underlying motivation, we would find that he experienced a great deal of trouble in his life because of his sloppy work. He wants Ryan to avoid those same problems, so he tries to help him be more careful in his work by pointing out his carelessness. There is certainly nothing wrong with his motives, but his effort to meet that goal isn't working very well.

Dad isn't the only one with repeated responses. Ryan continues to respond to each new task with carelessness and little energy. The underlying thought in Ryan's response is this: "It doesn't matter how good a job I do; Dad will always find fault." Ryan feels there is no point in expending much energy because the outcome is always the same: criticism.

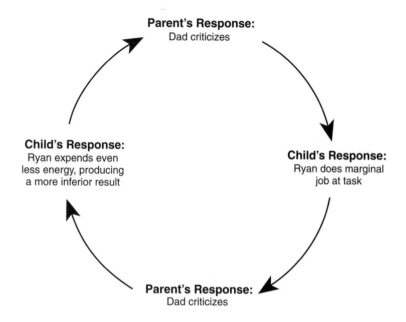

The underlying motivations and the subsequent responses produce a pattern that creates conflict between Ryan and his dad. Because Dad loves Ryan, he can't ignore Ryan's poor work, so he continues to do what he thinks will encourage Ryan to improve. Ryan sees no point in trying harder because more effort doesn't change the outcome. Each cycle

Each cycle through the pattern increases the strain.

through the pattern increases the strain between the father and son, and their rut gets deeper. The key is to recognize their pattern and to help them change their responses. This will not be an easy task because Dad believes Ryan's behavior would worsen even more if he stopped criticizing him, and Ryan is too discouraged to put much effort into changing. Without a change by one or both of them they will remain in this frustrating rut.

Parents must look beyond the immediate circumstances and change their repeated responses. Impossible? No, not at all.

Changing the pattern occurs through four understandable steps.

Step 1: Recognize parent-child patterns
Step 2: Clarify responsibility
Step 3: Make a plan that changes your response
Step 4: Evaluate and modify the plan

First, I will help you understand these four steps. Then I will show you how to use these steps to change the seven most common and destructive parent-child patterns.

By the time you have finished reading this book, you can expect to

1. Recognize the seven frequently occurring parent-child patterns that produce and perpetuate family difficulties
2. Understand why the patterns continue to operate in families through many generations
3. Determine which patterns may be operating in your family
4. Clarify your parental responsibilities and eliminate false guilt that parents so often carry
5. Clarify your children's responsibilities and recognize how your children may be avoiding them
6. Develop a plan to change the repetitive patterns that cause family tension
7. Develop greater understanding of your spouse and children through discussion questions frequently asked in counseling sessions

8. See how God has worked in other families and realize that he is lovingly interested and vigorously working in your family

Patterns are present in every family; it is your job as a parent to become aware of them. I am reminded of the biblical story of Elisha and his servant. The servant was frightened because of the army that had gathered against them:

> Now when the attendant of the man of God had risen early and gone out, behold, an army with horses and chariots was circling the city. And his servant said to him, "Alas, my master! What shall we do?"
> So he [Elisha] answered, "Do not fear, for those who are with us are more than those who are with them."
> Then Elisha prayed and said, "O LORD, I pray, open his eyes that he may see." And the LORD opened the servant's eyes, and he saw; and behold, the mountain was full of horses and chariots of fire all around Elisha.
>
> 2 Kings 6:15–17

Even though the horses and chariots of fire were present, the servant didn't see them. Like Elisha's servant, may God open our eyes to see. May we see the destructive parent-child patterns present in our homes. In the next chapter, we will examine some ways of recognizing our repetitive responses.

2

Haven't We
Been Here Before?

Step 1: Recognize the Pattern

I suppose my expectations for what should occur on a family vacation are unreasonably high. When our daughter Melissa was almost two years old we went on a family trip. The drive to the hotel went smoothly. Everyone enjoyed the day's activities. Nothing major was spilled at the restaurant. The room was comfortable, and everyone had settled down for a good night's rest. We made it through the first day!

I awakened in the middle of the night feeling very ill, and soon knew I either had the flu or a touch of food poisoning. After spending some intense moments in the bathroom, I crawled on my hands and knees back to bed. For about thirty minutes I had been making various noises of some magnitude, including knocking over a box of toys on my return crawl. I was pleased–sort of–that I had awakened no one. As I lay down, Melissa quietly coughed and rolled over. Bonnie immediately sat straight up in bed and said, "Check Melissa to see if she's all right." At that moment I experienced an obvious example of selective attention. Even though Bonnie was asleep, she was still attending to Melissa. It didn't appear that she was attending to me. Obviously Bonnie can't care for everything, and some things are more important to notice. I am generally self-sufficient, or at least more so than our two year old. It isn't usually necessary for Bonnie to pay attention to my nighttime activities, so she doesn't.

When patterns are being formed we pay attention to them. When they are established and we have reached a certain level of comfort with them, they stop demanding our conscious attention. They continue to operate, but on an autopilot level. To change, we need to pull these patterns back into our consciousness and take them off autopilot.

The simplest and most direct way of gaining information about our repetitive behaviors is to ask others. Asking for feedback about a specific area of your life will help you recognize your patterns of response. I might ask, "Bonnie, am I too harsh when I correct a mistake the kids make?" Asking someone about one of your patterns is simple but not easy. Before asking, it would be helpful to answer the following questions yourself.

Questions to Consider

1. Do I really want to know?
2. Am I ready to listen without becoming defensive?
3. What will I do with the information?
4. What areas do I need to take off autopilot?
5. Am I ready to change my patterns?
6. Who would answer the question honestly and give me constructive feedback? (2 Chron. 18:5–34).

Let's look at five different ways of understanding our repeated responses.

1. Consider Your Beliefs

Biblical directives and principles were given to be followed. As parents we may hold quite firmly to rules we believe are scriptural, thinking we are being true to our faith. Because the scriptural teaching and the commandments are divinely inspired we can easily slip into believing that our parental rules also have divine inspiration. When this occurs we don't have the freedom to modify our responses. Furthermore, our rigid adherence to certain rules, ironically, can push our children into behavior that is inconsistent with the Scriptures.

Our parental rules and responses that are meant to teach the biblical directives may be effective or ineffective. Linda and Kent want their daughter Tammy to refrain from premarital sex. They feel they have solid backing from the seventh commandment concerning adultery and from other biblical teaching that limits sexual intercourse to the marital relationship. As a result of this teaching and their spiritual commitment, they decide to set her dating age at sixteen. Tammy finds this very distasteful but abides by it. As soon as she is allowed to date, however, she begins to do so with great gusto, due to her resentment and built-up frustration, and she violates the commandment. The dating rule was meant to achieve a divine purpose but unfortunately had the opposite effect.

Reexamine Scripture, your beliefs, and your responses to make sure they are biblical and effective.

Questions to Consider

1. What rules do you have in your family that are based directly on Scripture?
2. Why do you think they are based on Scripture?
3. Does your spouse agree with each rule? With its basis?

4. Is each rule meeting its purpose?
5. Does your child know the purpose of each rule?
6. Would altering some rules accomplish the same goals, with fewer disagreements?

2. Understand Your Underlying Motivation

Our repeated responses are usually focused on meeting our individual and family needs. If we can identify the need, we can more easily see how it influences our behavior. When we understand the need, we can change a negative rut by finding new ways to meet the need—a recycled response. Let's look at a brief conversation in one family.

Bill and Mary frequently argue with their sixteen-year-old daughter Stacey about Eric, her current boyfriend.

Mom says to Stacey, "One of the things I don't like is the way he talks to you. I don't approve of his language. Besides, you used to make up your own mind and now you do whatever he tells you."

"Don't blame him for what I do, I make up my own mind. And that's the way everyone talks—this is the '90s. Besides, talk isn't everything. He loves me and treats me well."

Dad comments, "I guess I missed the time he treated you well. If he did, I would think he'd get you home by your curfew."

"Dad, that wasn't his fault! We were with Todd and Amy and Todd had to drop her off first. Eric told him that I needed to be home by midnight, but Eric wasn't the driver and he couldn't help it."

Mom (still bothered by his language) states, "He makes a very poor impression by the way he talks . . . and by the way he looks. Does he have to wear his hair that way?"

"Mom, you would like him if you just got to know him. You don't even know him, so how can you judge him?"

Dad, trying to make his final point, says, "Stacey, you are a bright, talented, and beautiful young woman. You can do better than Eric; he just isn't good enough for you. We are not going to allow you to see him any longer."

Stacey shouts, "I love him and you can't stop me from seeing him!"

The parents emphasize Eric's negative points and Stacey counters by defending each one. The more critical the parents are of Eric the more Stacey defends him as her only true love. Stacey thus commits herself even more to Eric–the opposite of what the parents think is best for her. The discussion turns into a power struggle with each side more and more committed to winning.

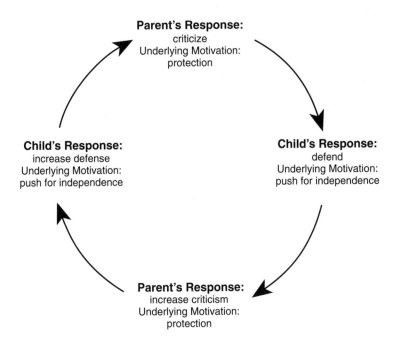

Parent's Response:
criticize
Underlying Motivation:
protection

Child's Response:
defend
Underlying Motivation:
push for independence

Parent's Response:
increase criticism
Underlying Motivation:
protection

Child's Response:
increase defense
Underlying Motivation:
push for independence

Underlying Force

Clearly the focus is on Eric's lack of admirable qualities, but what are the individual needs in this situation? Either parent may have a strong need to control Stacey or to protect her from the pitfalls involved in the dating scene. Stacey resents the overcontrolling stance and has a need to show her parents that they can't run her life. She is in control and will do what she pleases.

Recycled Response

Bill and Mary want Stacey to find a new boyfriend, but the repeated response of finding fault—with Stacey defending Eric—isn't working. If they ask Stacey to tell them about Eric—with an emphasis on his positive points rather than his negative ones—some real communication may occur. Her parents may discover that Stacey has already considered certain problems in dating someone like Eric. Stacey would feel better about her parents if they would take the time to find out why she likes Eric. Bill and Mary may even come to appreciate some of Eric's qualities. An open conversation may convince the parents to be less controlling and protective and provide Stacey less reason to rebel.

To hold Stacey accountable, her parents could discuss one or two of their concerns with her and request that she come up with a plan to address their apprehension—making it in by curfew would be an excellent place to start.

This family was attempting to meet legitimate needs, but their repeated responses were leaving the family at a dead end. New responses may not be ideal but they will help the family to get unstuck.

Questions to Consider

1. What are some of your important needs that you continually strive to meet?

2. How do these needs influence your patterns of response?
3. What needs do other members in your family seek to meet?

3. Examine Your Parents' Example

At Christmas I hate the statement on a box that reads, "Some assembly required." This usually means it will be at least New Year's Day before the item will be ready for use. I usually end up wanting a few private moments with the person who wrote the accompanying directions. They always look very clear but are totally unrelated to the parts in my hand—or else are meant for someone much smarter than I am. After several frustrating attempts at following the instructions, I usually hunt for the box and look at the picture. Only when I study what the end product looks like can I figure out how to assemble it.

We consult the picture and often do what was done in our families of origin.

Recognizing some of our patterns can be a difficult task. A dominant influence on our parental behavior is the picture in our minds of the way our parents reared us. This picture may not be what works to produce emotionally healthy children, but it is nevertheless the picture we have. So when a particular situation comes up, as parents we consciously or subconsciously consult the picture and often do what was done in our families of origin. This pattern of behavior can either foster positive interactions or prevent needed changes.

Is modeling really that powerful an influence on the way we act? To answer this question, let's look at several Scripture passages and a personal experience.

Positive modeling is certainly advocated as an effective way of teaching when we consider how

- Moses advised parents to teach their children through modeling–Deuteronomy 6:6–9
- Jesus taught his disciples by setting the example–John 13:14–15
- Paul encouraged Timothy to teach others by being an example–1 Timothy 4:12

We also find negative modeling in Scripture. Genesis tells about four generations of Jacob's family. This family modeled a coping style of being deceitful in difficult circumstances.

Jacob's grandfather Abraham was fearful that the Egyptians would kill him in order to take his beautiful wife, Sarah, for themselves. He therefore, on separate occasions, deceived Pharaoh and Abimelech by saying that Sarah was his sister (12:11–13; 20:2, 11–13).

Jacob's father, Isaac, was fearful that he would be killed by the men of Gerar because his wife, Rebekah, was beautiful. Like Abraham, he deceived Abimelech, saying Rebekah was his sister (26:7).

Jacob and his mother, Rebekah, deceived Isaac so Jacob could receive the blessing meant for the firstborn (27:5–29).

Rebekah deceived Isaac to secure protection for Jacob (27:42–46).

Jacob's Uncle Laban deceived Jacob by giving him Leah in marriage instead of Rachel (29:18–25).

Jacob deceived Laban by leaving without notice (31:17–21).

Rachel deceived Laban by stealing his idols (31:34).

Jacob's sons Simeon and Levi deceived Shechem and Hamor to gain revenge on them for raping their sister Dinah (34:13).

Jacob's sons deceived him concerning Joseph's disappearance and the destruction of his tunic (37:31–34).

Joseph deceived his brothers about his identity (42:7).

None of these successive sets of parents sat down with their children and lectured them on the fine points of deception. The parents simply modeled this style of coping and the children learned it. The pattern of the parents became the pattern of the children.

Last summer while mowing the lawn, I noticed a short individual following me, pushing a toy lawn mower. After a while I felt hot, so I took off my shirt. As I made the next round the short person was also shirtless. Now I didn't tell my son Brian to mow the lawn or to take off his shirt. He just saw what I was doing and imitated my actions.

The example set by our parents is very influential on our own behavior. If the picture provided by your parents is rather negative, you may be spending much time and energy being angry at them for the poor example they provided. Perhaps your parents did the best job they knew how to do. Blaming them won't change your behavior, but being aware of their modeling allows you to consciously follow their example or to change the family picture.

Consider how the family patterns you inherited influence your behavior in four important areas.

Questions to Consider

Communication

1. How did your parents communicate with each other and with you and your siblings?
2. Do you and your spouse talk about your feelings with each other?
3. Do your children generally talk with you about how they feel or must they show you by their actions?

Affection

1. How did your parents show affection to each other and to you and your siblings?
2. How affectionate are you and your spouse around your children?
3. How do you let your children know you love them? That you like them?

Anger

1. How did your parents act when they were angry?
2. How do you and your spouse express your anger?
3. Can your children talk about their anger or can they only show you they are angry by their behavior?

Problem Resolution

1. How did your parents resolve problems?
2. Do family conflicts get resolved in your home or only swept under the rug?
3. What conflicts are you avoiding?

4. Study Your Roles

We enjoy certain plays, movies, or television shows because we appreciate, identify with, or despise some of the roles the actors portray. As a parent you also have a definite part, or role, that you perform in your family. Can you identify your role(s)?

One of my roles is the Fixer. From my father's modeling, I learned that most objects around the house are fixable. I get a lot of attention and praise in my family for my repair work.

How do I know when the flapper in the toilet reservoir isn't working and the water is running through? I know the sound it makes, and I listen for it because that is something I can fix. When I fix something, Bonnie usually says, "You are pretty handy. I think we'll keep you around." I like that.

One Saturday afternoon she called for me in her something-is-broken voice. I went to the kitchen and found a Tupperware glass stuck upside down in the drain of the sink. I tried several times to pull the glass out, but was unsuccessful because of the suction created by greasy water that had collected, which also made the glass slippery. On my third attempt Mike came into the kitchen; he asked several times if he could try. Before I tell you how I responded, you must keep in mind that fixing things in the family is *my* role. I don't like other people infringing on my territory! Well, Mike insisted on helping. While I was drying my hands to get a tool I needed from the garage, I reluctantly gave him an opportunity to help. He helped all right—he pulled the glass out on his first attempt. It felt like the Sword in the Stone story. Bonnie was pleased with Mike's success. Mike was proud of himself that he did something Dad couldn't do. And I was annoyed that he got the credit I usually get.

Identify Your Roles

As a parent you must be able to identify your role(s). Why is this critical? Are they really that important? Yes, roles limit our ability to modify our repeated responses.

For example, Dad has a role of being the Drill Sergeant. His role dictates his behavior. What he says is the law, and it is not permissible to question his authority or his directives. Now, teenagers somehow get the idea that they should run their own lives. A son or daughter will find a way to let Dad know he can't control everything. One way of doing that is to defy him by getting into trouble. The adolescent may very well have good morals but will do something to let Dad know that he isn't omnipotent. The problem evolves in direct response to Dad's role.

You can well imagine that when Dad sees the defiance his role will dictate a firm response. He becomes more domineering, meting out longer grounding, more punishment, and loss of additional privileges. His role keeps the family in a negative circular pattern: The harsher Dad becomes, the more rebellious the teenager will become, causing Dad to be even harsher. The way out of this circular pattern is to talk about what is happening, but Dad's role will allow neither conversation nor negotiation. The role keeps the family caught in a negative rut.

Roles limit our ability to modify our repeated responses.

Single moms sometimes look for a stepdad for their children who will provide firm discipline. The Discipliner usually has difficulty being close and affectionate with his stepchildren since that behavior is inconsistent with his role.

As soon as a woman becomes pregnant, she is taught that she must take care of herself. Everyone nags her to eat right, to see the doctor regularly, to take her vitamins, to get enough rest, and not to do too much strenuous work. Why does all this fuss occur? It happens because Mom is no longer just taking care of herself. She is now the protector of this baby. Everyone concerned reinforces her role as the Protector. If she does a good job of protecting, we call her a Good Mom. During the pregnancy and over the years she pours a lot of effort, love, tears, and prayers into protecting her child. When her child is safe and doing well, Mom feels good about herself.

However, when adolescence hits, the rules of motherly protection change. Society, her husband, and certainly the adolescent, who seems to want to be a kamikaze pilot, now tell Mother to allow her child to expose himself to more dangerous situations. What we once rewarded Mom for we tell her to stop doing. Mom is now labeled overprotective, controlling, and interfering.

When adolescence hits, the rules of motherly protection change.

When this predictable shift occurs, two problems can emerge. (1) How can Mom turn loose her protective role and allow the adolescent permission to experiment? Her fear for her child makes it difficult to change what she has been doing for years. But if Mom doesn't make the shift, the adolescent will push harder and act more outrageously to gain release from her protection. (2) How can Mom find other ways to feel good about herself? Relinquishing her protective role will make her feel less needed and can decrease her self-esteem. Compounding the self-esteem problem may be the shortage of other areas to which she can look for success. She may not have kept her job skills current because of her involvement with her children. The marriage is okay, but may not be dazzling because of all the family demands. Thus her need to feel good about herself can keep her locked into her protective role.

The solution to this change in role is not an easy one. Anticipating the switch from the Protector to the Supporter is most helpful. Mothers who have found other interests that utilize their skills and strengths go through this transition with less pain. Keeping the marriage strong is also a good way to avoid the empty nest difficulties. Moms need support from their husbands to make this transition. Criticizing her for being overprotective is counterproductive for both Mom and the adolescent, and for the marriage.

Frequently there is a connection between a parent's vocation and the way he or she interacts with the children. For eight or more hours a day the job role is reinforced. The role works well there, so it is easy to bring that role home. For example, a law enforcement officer may tend to "police" his or her children. How do the children get the parent's attention? Behaving properly might work, but sometimes children feel they don't get the approval they want by positive behavior. The next best thing is to get negative attention. The children have learned that if they get to the Cop they also get to the parent.

So, if a parent is a

Police Officer—breaking the law will get attention
Teacher—flunking will get attention
Family Counselor—family arguments or sibling fights will
    get attention
Pastor—public immorality or drunkenness will get attention
Banker—squandering money, bad credit, or being broke
    will get attention
Military Sergeant or Officer—disobeying will get attention

These negative behaviors are certainly generalizations, but they do work to gain a parent's attention. So, parents, think about how your role at work makes you successful and consider how it works at home.

Change Ineffective Roles

To make changes in your role, you must know your role, the environmental and emotional cues that prompt it, and the needs met through it. When you are aware of these you can decide where it works for you. Make sure you function in your role in those places. And decide where it doesn't work for you. If you decide to stop using the role there, what will you do differently? It will be very easy to fall back into the old role if you don't have an alternate plan clearly in mind.

If you find that your role is beneficial at work and limiting at home, make sure you leave it at work. Build in a transition from work to home so that you have time to change mental gears. This may be accomplished by spending a few minutes on the way home mentally finishing work-related matters. If possible, you might take a few minutes by yourself when you arrive home before interacting with your family. You also must choose to ignore certain cues that normally prompt the old role response and choose to respond differently to other cues.

> ## Build in a transition from work to home so that you have time to change mental gears.

Identify the need that your role meets for you and for the family. The Drill Sergeant takes care of the need for structure and rules, for example. However, the role limits closeness and family unity. So, determine other ways of meeting structure and rule needs. Instead of Dad being the Drill Sergeant, let Mom be more firm in setting limits for the children. Then Dad isn't always the bad guy. Modify your role or your spouse's so that together they blend to meet your children's needs. Know that your role may need to change over time to match your child's development (such as from Protector to Supporter).

Questions to Consider

1. What are your parental roles? What are those of your spouse's?
2. What behaviors are associated with each of your roles?

3. How do the roles reinforce repetitive responses?
4. How would your family be different without these roles? (Usually there would be improvement in some aspects and problems in other areas.)
5. Would the new or recycled responses contradict your role?

5. Check Your Relationships

Whose side are you on? Who is on your side? You may not have thought about sides in your family, but taking sides is a major component in keeping your family stuck in negative parent-child ruts. Your family quite likely divides into sides for activities, places to eat, arguments, decisions, and styles of coping. Sides are also taken based on personality, sex, and birth order.

There is usually a pattern to the way sides are taken. If you observe carefully, you will probably see the pattern in the way your family takes sides. Maybe you're not convinced that taking sides is that big of a concern at your house. But do any of these sound familiar?

You always pick on me.
Why does he always get his way?
She did the same thing yesterday but you didn't ground her.
Why do I have to do everything around here?
You like him better than me.
Why does he get more privileges than I do, when I'm older?
You're just not being fair.
Dad and I never talk.
Mom and Dad can go for weeks without talking to each other.
Nobody likes me. I don't belong in this family.

Do you ever see

- Intense sibling conflict from favoritism and the jealousy that results
- Disobedience of children because of parents' disagreement on the rules or on the consequences of breaking the rules
- Hurt feelings because nonresident Dad gives birthday gifts to one child and forgets the others' birthdays
- A runaway child who feels he or she doesn't belong in the family
- Parents' separation due to disagreements over dealing with the children

Any of these could be the result of taking sides in the family.

The extent of advantages gained through taking sides depends on the members of the side. A child's power is much greater if he sides with a parent rather than with another sibling. Isaac's and Jacob's families provide excellent examples of the advantages and disadvantages of taking sides. When sides are taken, the following effects often occur. Are any of these taking place in your family?

Taking Sides Provides Safety and Protection

There is less risk involved in talking to someone who is on your side rather than on the opposing side. By definition, being on the same team suggests more support and less criticism. Taking sides can offer physical safety as well. In families where sexual molestation has occurred, the females may form a side against the males as a way of feeling safe and nurtured.

Esau was so angry at Jacob for obtaining the firstborn's blessing that he made plans to kill him. Rebekah protected Jacob by removing him from the scene and preventing Esau's plans (Gen. 27:41–28:6). A generation later, Jacob took precautions to protect his favorite son, Joseph, by placing him in the safest spot in the caravan (33:1–2).

Taking Sides Brings Closeness and Belonging

Being on the same side or team allows people to feel close and to experience a sense of belonging. At some point in our lives, many of us have experienced the rejection associated with being picked last or not at all. The bond with Rebekah provided Jacob with a close relationship in the family (25:28). Joseph's father gave him a tunic, a symbol of his father's favor (37:3).

Taking Sides Gains Extra Privileges

When a child sides with one parent, that parent may grant extra privileges or exemptions from certain punishments or restrictions. The child, of course, enjoys this favoritism. If the other parent voices some concerns about the first parent's inconsistency, he or she may be viewed as being too harsh. This reinforces the child's positive feelings toward the favoring parent, as well as his or her negative feelings toward the other parent, further polarizing the sides.

Jacob received no discipline for his deception of Isaac because Rebekah protected him. She assured him that she would personally deal with any consequences that might result from the deception (27:13).

Taking Sides Increases Power

When people unite they obtain more power. Two adults should certainly be stronger than one child, regardless of the child's age or size. If your child frequently gets his or her way, you have a power leak. A child simply cannot have more strength than two adults unless one (or both) is sharing power with the child. Enough power can be siphoned from the parents for the child to exert control. I have seen a six year old who is barely four feet tall bark orders to both his college-educated parents. I have also seen a six-foot-five-inch football player immediately obey his five-foot-two-inch mother without question. Jacob had enough power to obtain the first-born's blessing only with Rebekah's assistance (27:5–10).

This transfer of power from the parents usually occurs because one or both parents allow or encourage the child to behave in a way that defies a stated rule. Jason's parents say they aren't going to tolerate any speeding tickets, for example, but Dad frequently asks his son if the new car has blown everything else off the road. Jason gets the idea that prestige is more important than the fear of getting tickets. With Dad's encouragement, he speeds more and worries less.

Taking Sides Gives Access to More Information

Usually people share information more freely with those on the same side. Out of frustration, Mom may share her concern or hurt with her daughter about disagreements with

> **If your child frequently gets his or her way, you have a power leak.**

Dad. This may temporarily help Mom feel better, but the daughter may then use the information to her benefit at a time of her choosing. This sharing of information also erodes the daughter's relationship with Dad. Rebekah gave Jacob the information about Isaac's plan concerning the firstborn's blessing (27:6–8). Even though it caused great family tension, Jacob used the information for his personal gain.

Taking Sides Predetermines Responses

A person who takes a side is expected to be loyal and to support the side's position. Rebekah was quite insistent that Jacob comply with her wishes (27:8, 13). He would have lost favor with her if he hadn't agreed to the deception.

41

Being on opposite sides prevented Joseph and his brothers from getting along. Each brother pressured the others into shunning Joseph. If one of them had tried to befriend Joseph, he would have been accused of being disloyal.

Taking Sides Prevents Resolution

To maintain unity and to be in a position of mutual support, people on the same side may deny or avoid difficulties that exist in their relationships. Those on opposite sides also hesitate to cross the gap because the enemy is not to be trusted, and good-faith negotiation never occurs.

Being on opposite sides, Esau and Jacob had little chance to resolve their problems, much less become friends. Even after twenty years Jacob still worried about how Esau would respond to him (32:6–7). In the next generation, taking sides prevented the resolution of differences between Joseph and his brothers. Years later in Egypt the brothers were frightened of Joseph and what he might do to them (45:3–5).

Taking Sides Prevents Learning
New Coping Skills

Instead of personally developing new coping skills, people learn to rely on others on the same side for protection. When a child sides with one parent, the child quickly learns that the parent will deal with those on the opposite side. Thus the child doesn't learn how to cope with the situation himself. Jacob didn't have to figure out how to deal with Esau because Rebekah whisked him away to live with Uncle Laban (27:43).

Taking Sides Creates Jealousy

Jealousy because of favoritism is likely to occur between siblings who are on opposite sides. Esau was very jealous that

Jacob received the blessing and he vowed to kill him (27:41). Joseph's brothers became so angry and jealous of him that they planned to kill him (37:19–35). Jealousy also may occur between parents as they compete for the child's loyalty. And whoever is on the opposite side has little chance of developing a positive relationship with that child.

Taking Sides Regulates Communication

Taking sides governs communication by determining who can talk to whom and what can be discussed. The parent who is allied with the child usually speaks for the child to the other parent.

Isaac and Esau communicated, and Rebekah and Jacob communicated. Rebekah did talk to her husband on occasion, but for the purpose of gaining an advantage for Jacob.

Taking Sides Regulates Problem-Solving Approaches

Family members will separate into their respective sides, especially in times of high stress. This polarized position limits objectivity, brainstorming of ideas, and negotiation of solutions.

The best way to overcome the problems associated with taking sides is to build the relationship between Mom and Dad and then make connections with those children on the opposite side.

Questions to Consider

1. What problems occurred in your family of origin as a result of taking sides?
2. How did your parents deal with them?
3. What hindered you from assisting someone on the opposite side?

43

4. Could you contact that person now? Would (s)he accept your support or friendship now?
5. How does taking sides in your present family limit your ability to modify your repeated responses?
6. How does taking sides limit the development of solutions in your family?
7. Does jealousy create friction in your family?
8. Can you support each family member?
9. Do you or others try to compensate for the unfairness associated with favoritism? For example, if Aunt, Grandma, or the other parent buys his or her favorite child a gift, do you then buy a gift for the child who didn't receive one? How effective is this in solving the problem? Can you think of any better solutions?

Our lack of conscious awareness, our beliefs, our underlying motivations, our parents' examples, our roles, and our relationships can keep us trapped in repeating responses. As you think about your responses, one of the issues to be addressed is, Do my parental responses need to change? Your answer ultimately depends on how well you think your responses work. Over time, responses work well if the appropriate level of responsibility is assumed. If you assume too little responsibility, eventually you will get burned with negative consequences. If you assume too much responsibility, you will be tired, burned out, and angry. What are your parenting responsibilities? Let's proceed to chapter 3 to find out.

3

Is All of This Up to Me?

Step 2: Clarify Responsibility

Control and Responsibility

I can't control everything concerning my children. At times this really scares me. Practically speaking, this means there are no iron-clad guarantees; parenting theories won't yield 100 percent positive results. No parent is immune from heartache.

Many of our repeated responses are attempts to make our children make what we think is the right decision. Yet God is solidly committed to individuals making their own choices, so this parental limitation concerning control is here to stay.

Control and responsibility are closely linked. I can't control the weather, so I am not responsible for the rain. I can control whether I make it to work on time, so I am accountable for my punctuality. God has provided direction for the distribution of husbands' and wives' responsibilities (Eph. 5:22–32). Concerning parents and children, we read that children are to be responsible for obedience, while fathers are to be responsible for discipline and instruction. Fathers are to also avoid provoking their children to anger (Eph. 6:1–4). Assuming responsibilities assigned to others is destructive in relationships, so focus on your duties and allow your child to do the same.

Who's Responsible?

	Pre-decision	Decision	Post-decision
Parent's Responsibility	Present rules Monitor situation Help child understand his or her feelings Clarify consequences Observe child	No parental responsibility (except to pray)	Enforce consequences Support through consequences Congratulate positive outcomes
Child's Responsibility	Listen Ask questions Understand feelings Understand consequences	Make decisions	Face consequences Feel good about positive outcomes Take credit for successes

As an example of specific parental responsibilities, we have an excellent model in how God dealt with Cain. From Genesis 4:3–15 we know that Cain's offering was unacceptable to God, making Cain very angry. Let's consider how God responded to Cain's anger.

1. God dealt with him in four sentences (not a long lecture); he asked Cain to examine his feelings and to consider the consequences (both positive and negative). God observed what occurred.
2. At the point of decision God didn't force Cain to do the right thing, though he felt disappointment and displeasure about the decision Cain made.

3. When Cain killed his brother, God held him accountable for his actions and he supported Cain through the
   consequences.

God didn't make Cain's decisions for him. Neither should
we try to make our children's decisions for them. We are not
in control of their decisions. And remember, if you don't
have control, you don't have responsibility (or guilt).

The dilemma of determining our parental responsibilities
is made even more difficult by children who would at times
be glad to give all of the responsibility to us. Asking this question will help sort it out: "Whose decision is this?" Children,
and adults too, sometimes want other people to make their
decisions for them.

In junior high school, my best friend was Bruce. When I
spent the weekend with him we would ride our bikes around
town exploring. One day Bruce took me to one of his great
finds, a pet monkey. I am not sure that he really was a pet,
but he nevertheless was a monkey. Now this was a dirty,
ornery critter who would bite if given the chance. He
wouldn't bite immediately, but would wait until you thought
he could be trusted. Of course by that time you were holding him, so he could get a really good bite. Even though he
had many disgusting traits, he was the only monkey we knew,
so we would let him climb on us while trying to keep him
from removing parts of our bodies.

Whenever I hear the expression "the monkey on your
back" I always think of that ill-tempered little rascal. If the
monkey is on your back, it means that you have assumed
responsibility for the situation. You may be trying to figure
out how to reach a goal, work through complications, or fit
things together. Other family members who are without the
monkey on their backs don't feel the pressure. They are at
liberty to relax, sit back, and watch how the person with the
monkey is going to solve the dilemma.

Families always encounter problems when one person constantly carries the monkey. That overly responsible person becomes burdened down and frustrated with his or her limited power to accomplish the goals. Those who are less responsible don't learn to cope, thus missing the rewards of responsibility.

If the monkey is on your back, it means that you have assumed responsibility for the situation.

Because family members pass the monkey back and forth, it is crucial to know who has the monkey. He should be on the back of the person who is legitimately the responsible party. Some adolescents make a fine art of "monkey passing." They are pros at giving the monkey to their parents and avoiding accountability. Here are some statements that usually mean the monkey is headed your way. Following each monkey-passing statement is a suggested parental response to return the monkey to the child.

The Fine Art of Monkey Passing

Adolescent Says	Adolescent Implies	Parent's Response
"I forgot."	*I didn't do it on purpose, so don't be too hard on me.*	"It's too bad you forgot, because doing it now is probably inconvenient for you, but please go do it now."
"I didn't know that was the rule."	*It's your fault because you didn't tell me about the rule. So I should receive no punishment.*	"It's unfortunate that you keep forgetting the rules. You might check the list on the refrigerator to help keep those rules fresh in your mind."

48

Adolescent Says	Adolescent Implies	Parent's Response
		Hopefully the extra chore that you now have to do will help you remember next time."
"That isn't the rule!"	*It's your fault because you weren't clear on the fine points of the rule.*	"Perhaps I was unclear. I want to make sure that I am clear now. You will not be allowed to go out until you have the history report completed."
"Nobody in my whole school has to follow that rule! This is the '90s!"	*You are outdated and out of touch with what other good parents are doing. Justify the rule!*	"I have this rule because I think it is in your best interest. Show me how we can come up with a different rule that will still serve your best interest. Until you can do that, we will stick with the current rule."
"I'm not following that rule."	*So what are you going to do about it?*	"It will be tough for you if you choose to disobey that rule because you will lose your weekend privileges." (It would be good to walk away at this point because there is no use arguing about the issue. It is now the child's decision and there is nothing more that you can do. Just be consistent with the consequences.)

(continued)

(The Fine Art of Monkey Passing—continued)

Adolescent Says	Adolescent Implies	Parent's Response
"I did what you said."	*I did what I was told to do, so it's your fault because you didn't communicate clearly.*	"Apparently I didn't communicate clearly. What I meant for you to do was this, so please do it now."
"I know you don't believe me, but I did my assignment and I lost it."	*You never trust me.* (This diverts focus from job not done to why you never believe her.)	"I'm sorry you lost your work. However, our agreement was that you do your homework and I let you go to the dance. When you show me your work, I will be glad to follow through on my part of the bargain."
"I did it last time. It's her turn to do it."	*Prove who did it last before I will do it now.*	"I don't know who did it last. I just need to have it done now. Will you help me?" Or, "I don't know who did it last. Will you work out a way for us to keep track of that? But for now, I need you to do it."
"I did *almost* all of what you said. Can't I go now?"	*Be glad for what I did do and reward me or I won't even do that much next time.*	"Our deal was that you finish your job and then I take you to the movie. I am ready to take you as soon as you are finished."
"I promise I will finish when I get back."	*Believe me, and give me what I want.* (You must decide if "I promise" is an acceptable reason	"I am willing to try it this time but I'm expecting you to keep your promise. If this doesn't work, I won't compromise again." Or, if you have been

Adolescent Says	Adolescent Implies	Parent's Response
	to let her go. Generally the rule I follow is this: first the work and then the benefits, because that is the way the world operates—my paycheck comes when my work is completed.)	burned by broken promises, "When you finish, I will be glad to take you."
"I couldn't do my homework because I was doing the dishes and cleaning the house."	*It is your fault because you made me do the housework.*	"Sounds like you are having difficulty managing your time. Would you like me to help with your time management, or do you think you can work it out on your own?"
"I'm sorry. It won't happen again."	*I apologized, now get off my case and leave me alone.*	"I appreciate the apology, but you also need to complete your work. Please go finish it now."
"You never do anything around here. I am not going to do that. It's your turn."	*Justify what you want me to do based on what you do.*	"If you think things are unfair, we can sit down and talk about it. You come up with a list of chores that we could negotiate. But for now we need to get these things done. Please do what I asked."
"I don't want to do that. It's boring (or messy, or uncool)."	*Make it attractive so I want to do it. If you can't, I shouldn't have to do it.*	"You are certainly right. It is a messy job. After you are done, I will help you clean up." Or, "You are right about *(continued)*

51

(The Fine Art of Monkey Passing—continued)

Adolescent Says	Adolescent Implies	Parent's Response
		that. Do you want to trade for the one I am doing?"
"I didn't do anything wrong and I am not following your grounding."	*You can't punish me until you convince me that I did something wrong.*	"I am not going to argue about whether you disobeyed. I hope the grounding will give you some time to understand what you did wrong. You will be grounded until 7:00 A.M. Saturday."

In each of these situations, the adolescent has given the responsibility for the next move back to you. You may choose to

- Do what she wants you to do—justify what you said, meant, did, and so on. Your child then becomes the judge of how good an explanation you provided. You have now accepted the monkey.
- Pass the monkey back by holding the child accountable for her actions. You may give a brief explanation, but the focus must remain on her and her actions. If your child can shift the monkey back to you and keep it there, she has a chance to avoid her duties.

Questions to Consider

1. How do your children pass the monkey back to you?
2. How can you eliminate some of the ways your children make you responsible for their actions?
3. Is one parent being overly responsible and constantly carrying the monkey at your house?

We have established that as parents we can't control everything and that we should have our children make, and be responsible for, their own decisions. So what are our legitimate parental responsibilities?

Parental Responsibilities

Instead of repeating ineffective responses or continuing to push for control where you actually have none, focus on your responsibility of presenting, monitoring, and enforcing the rules that you believe your children should follow.

For example, most of us are law abiding citizens. Does society trust us to do what is best, without rules? No. The speed limit demonstrates this. Are you allowed to drive whatever speed you think appropriate? No, there are speed limit signs posted at certain intervals along streets and highways (rule presented). Unfortunately the posting of a speed limit sign doesn't adequately prevent speeding, so police officers patrol the roads to assure that people drive at the proper speed (rule monitored). When stopped, you may get a friendly reminder about the legal limit or you may get a ticket. If you persist in speeding, you will interact with the court system (rule enforced).

Some parents believe they must convince their children that a rule is a good rule and one they should follow. Consequently, they talk endlessly instead of following through on the stated consequences. If you were stopped three days in a row by the same police officer for exceeding the speed limit, what do you think would happen? I doubt that he would wring his hands, beg you to slow down, or lay a guilt trip on you. His monitoring job is not to convince you to follow the law. It is to hold you accountable. You may continue to drive faster than the law permits, and eventually you will pay higher fines and even lose your license. You may choose the point where you no longer wish to pay the consequences by simply following the rule. If society eliminated any one of these three—presenting, monitoring, enforcing—people would drive as fast as they pleased, making the road a dangerous place to be.

There is usually a pattern to the way rules break down. Some parents don't present the rules. Others do a great job of presenting the rules, but then don't monitor their child's behavior. Still others do quite well up to this point, but then don't enforce any consequences. Examine your rule pattern to determine where the breakdown occurs and what can be done to correct the problem.

Questions to Consider

1. How do you discipline for repeated offenses?
2. Do you try to convince your children to believe in a rule or to follow a rule?

Present Rules

Presenting the rules is a prerequisite for children's obedience. If you are having difficulty with your children following rules, sit down and go over the rules. Writing them down will clarify your expectations. God definitely experienced some of our parental struggles concerning rules when the children of Israel lapsed into idolatry (see Exodus 32). He was not pleased with their disobedience and gave the Ten Commandments a second time to emphasize their importance, writing them in stone. (It is probably sufficient to have ours written on paper and posted on the refrigerator.) Posting the rules prevents your children from passing the monkey to you because "You didn't tell me about the rules." Parents must present the rules if they expect their children to follow them.

For example, Samson wanted to marry a Philistine woman, which was against God's directives, and hence against his family's rule (see Exodus 34:12–16). How did Samson's parents present this rule concerning marriage? Did they refer to the rule, discuss the reasons for the rule, and expect obedience? Actually what they did was hope that Samson would follow the rule by enticing him to notice attractive Israelite women who would make excellent brides. They may have invited dozens of Israelite women to their house with the hope of finding one Samson might like. If that really did occur, where would you look for the monkey? Clearly, the parents own the monkey because they are trying to find ways of making Samson follow the rule.

Presentation Must Be Clear

Confusion about the rules leaves opportunity for manipulation. Parents must present the rules in terms that the child understands. If you tell your child, "Do not project yourself upward from your place of rest," she probably will miss the message about not jumping on her bed.

Writing down rules will clarify your expectations.

In Numbers 10:1–10, Moses explains to the Israelites what they were to do. If only one blast on a single trumpet was heard, the leaders were to assemble. If both trumpets were heard, the whole community was to assemble. In 1 Corinthians 14:8, Paul expands on the Numbers passage by stating, "If the bugle produces an indistinct sound, who will prepare himself for battle?" An unclear message will make it difficult for your children to understand and respond correctly. If your child misunderstands because you didn't explain the rule clearly, it keeps the monkey on your back.

Messages Must Not Be Mixed

A mixed message is one in which the various parts of the message, verbal and nonverbal, are inconsistent with each other. When you tell your child that you are serious about a rule (verbal part) your face should look serious (nonverbal part). It may confuse your child to have a casual look on your face or to use a tone of voice that isn't firm. When the situation is important and you are using words that are tentative and iffy your child may miss the significance of the rule or consequence. So when you talk with your child all parts of the presentation should be consistent.

Samson requested that his parents meet the Philistine woman. Perhaps wanting to avoid a scene, they went with Samson to Timnah. By doing so they gave Samson the message that it was probably okay after all to marry this woman. Why else would they have gone to Timnah but to check her out to see if she was acceptable? They wanted to say no verbally but they said yes by their actions, giving a mixed message about the importance of God's marital rule.

Questions to Consider

1. What are the rules in your family?
2. Who presents the rules?
3. How are the rules presented?
4. Is there agreement on what each rule really means (between spouses, between parents and child)?
5. Mixed messages are more likely to be given to children when parents aren't in agreement about the rule. On what rules do you and your spouse disagree?
6. What rules are most frequently broken?

Monitor Behavior

It won't work to tell your children what the rules are and then assume they will follow them. Do you always follow the posted speed limit? Doesn't the police officer keep you from going too fast at least some of the time? Children learn to obey rules because parents monitor their behavior and enforce the consequences of disobedience. As they grow and experience the rules they will begin to understand their importance and eventually will control their own behavior.

Behavior Must Be Compared to Rule

The rule is the guideline by which we measure the behavior. The police officer compares your speed with the posted speed. If you are going too fast, the officer will visit with you. The rule for your child is of no use if you don't refer to it in measuring her behavior. This comparison can be favorable (she obeyed) or unfavorable (she disobeyed). Frequently we pay more attention to the unfavorable comparison. Please keep in mind how special it is to your child when you comment on a favorable comparison.

You must compare your child's behavior with the stated rule.

Eli, an Old Testament priest, had two sons, Hophni and Phinehas. We assume that as a responsible priest and father he presented the rules to them concerning sacrifices, given in Leviticus 7:29–34. But when his sons blatantly disobeyed there is no record of his referring to the sacrificial rules (1 Sam. 2:22–25), even though it was an issue serious enough for God to remove his family from the priesthood (1 Sam. 2:28–29; 3:13).

Questions to Consider

1. Who monitors the rules in your family?

2. Does the same person present and monitor the rules? (Having more than one person involved requires good communication between spouses to prevent manipulation by the child.)
3. Is a fair comparison made between the rule and the behavior? How often does your mood influence this comparison?

Enforce Consequences

A parent can enforce a rule only if it has been clearly presented and adequately monitored. Rule enforcement also requires reasonable rules and parental unity. Consequences, furthermore, must be enforced consistently and as soon after the offense as possible. Make certain the consequences are enforceable and appropriate to the violation.

Consequences Should Be Consistent

Consistent enforcement of consequences confirms the rule and provides a sense of security for your child. Inconsistent enforcement teaches the child that the rule is trivial. She also learns to disbelieve what you say. Your mood, rather than the rule, becomes the measure of the child's behavior.

Consequences Should Be Timely

"When the sentence for a crime is not quickly carried out, the hearts of the people are filled with schemes to do wrong" (Eccles. 8:11 NIV). Imposing the consequence for the behavior as quickly as is possible establishes the connection between the misdeed and the disapproval. Waiting for two days or "until your father comes home" before responding weakens the connection and doesn't encourage the child to change her behavior. As this verse also indicates, delay can strengthen the commitment to do evil. Most of us don't jump from windows of tall buildings because the consequences of gravity are consistent and immediate.

Consequences Should Be Appropriate

If your child has trouble remembering the time limit on the phone, a consequence is in order. Two good, generic consequences would be loss of phone privileges for two days and cleaning out the garage. However, the loss of phone privileges for two days is more related to the problem, and much more likely to help your child control the amount of time spent on the phone.

Consequences Should Be Enforceable

Grounding a child to her room for thirteen years is an absurd consequence, because there is no way to enforce it.

It is better to impose a light consequence that you can enforce, rather than a heavy one that you cannot.

(Your child knows that, by the way.) A grounding of three days may be equally ridiculous if there are no parents home to enforce the restriction. It is better to impose a light consequence that you can enforce, rather than a heavy one that you cannot. Unenforceable consequences are the same as no consequences.

Consequences Should Be Positive

Children are more responsive to encouragement, praise, and rewards than they are to punishment. Praising them when they have followed a rule will do much more to establish that rule than will punishment when they have broken it. By the way, a reinforcer is something the children, not the adults, think is rewarding. Keep in mind that as children grow up, the rewards need to change. A young child might be pleased with a sticker on the fridge, a gummy worm, or a hug. Your high school student would probably prefer a later curfew or car privileges to a gummy worm! If you are unsure of what a good reward is, you can always ask your child. Children are usually eager to tell you what they want as a reward for good behavior.

Children are more responsive to encouragement, praise, and rewards than they are to punishment.

One powerful reinforcer is your attention. How do you do in this area? A common complaint in my office is that parents "always see me when I do something wrong, but they never see me do something right." When was the last time you caught your child doing something right? If you like something she is doing, say so!

If you like something she is doing, say so!

Bad behavior, if it is extreme enough, will command attention. If the only way children can get attention is by doing something bad, they will do something bad. Unfortunately, a child's negative behavior is often met with an equally negative response such as yelling and screaming, which actually reinforces the child's unacceptable behavior. Notice that the child is receiving the parent's attention—negative attention is better than no attention at all.

Questions to Consider

1. Who is in charge of enforcement at your house?
2. Do you and your spouse agree on who monitors and enforces various behaviors?

---

3. Is there consistency in your enforcement?
4. Who is the softy when enforcing consequences? Why?
5. Who never gives a break? What need does this meet for that parent?
6. Does your anger prompt you to threaten your child with more severe consequences than you can enforce? Than are fair?
7. What positive reinforcers do you use with your children for proper behavior?
8. What reinforcers would they like you to use?

Being aware of your patterns and then understanding which responsibilities are yours and which are your child's puts you in a position to change your repeated responses. In the next chapter, we will utilize this awareness and clarification of responsibility to develop a plan to modify the negative pattern.

4

You Have the Power to Change

Step 3: Make a Plan

In chapter 2 you recognized some of your repeated responses, and in chapter 3 you gained some clarity concerning your responsibilities. You now need a plan that will change your unproductive responses to a recycled response, as indicated in the diagram on the following page. Having a plan will break you out of the rut and place the monkey appropriately on the back of the responsible person.

I think I can hear some parents say, "You mean you want me to change my response (one that isn't that bad) in hopes that my children might change their responses (no guarantees). Are you crazy?"

Let's consider two concerns that make it difficult to change our responses. First, we generally don't think a change in *our* responses will bring about a change in *our child's* responses.

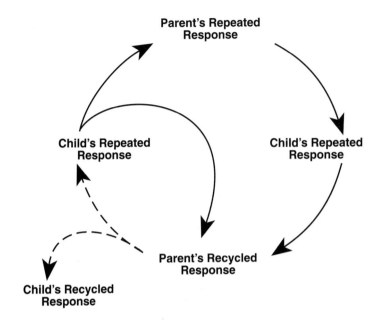

Second, we want the child to change first. If the child changes, we would be glad to change!

Will changing your response make that much of a difference? Can one person really change a situation? Here are some biblical examples where one person could have made a difference:

> Run to and fro through the streets of Jerusalem, and see now and take notice! Seek in her broad squares to see if you can find a man [as Abraham sought in Sodom], one who does justice, who seeks truth, sincerity and faithfulness; and I will pardon Jerusalem—for one uncompromisingly righteous person.
>
> Jeremiah 5:1 AMP

> And I searched for a man among them who should build up the wall and stand in the gap before Me for the land, that I should not destroy it; but I found no one.
>
> Ezekiel 22:30

One person would have made the difference. By changing your old pattern, you can make a difference. And you can make a difference in your family that will have a positive influence for generations to come.

The good news is you can change your part of the cycle—guaranteed!

The second concern, of course, is that we want our children to change first. (If they do change first, you are extremely blessed.) If the cycle has repeated itself several times, you can probably count on it not changing unless you change it. The good news is you can change your part of the cycle—guaranteed! That is your responsibility, and you can do it because it is under your control.

Determine the Goal

Be clear and very specific about what you want from your child. It is far better to state the goal positively, such as, "Please talk nicely to your sister," rather than, "Stop arguing with your sister." This allows you to monitor your children's interaction and make positive comments. You don't see the times when he stops himself from arguing, so you can't comment on it, but you can see and comment on the times he talks positively with his sister.

Develop a Plan

The plan needs to address two major issues. (1) You must develop and reinforce a new response. (2) You must prevent the old response from creeping in when you are angry or frustrated.

Determine a New Response

We will use Tommy's poor grades as an example. Tina, Tommy's mom, nags him about his homework, his assignments, and his grades. Tommy resents the nagging and has stopped doing the work. When he is forced to do it, he either loses it on the bus or doesn't turn it in. Tommy's dad, Larry, isn't very worried about his son's grades because he didn't do very well in school when he was a kid and he turned out okay.

Tina's repeated response to Tommy's poor grades is to ask every night after school if he has homework. Tina can't make Tommy bring home the appropriate books, study, or turn in the work. Continuing to nag him about those issues won't work as she doesn't have control over them.

Tina's new response may require several actions. She can make it easier for Tommy to study by limiting the distractions. I encourage parents to prohibit phone calls, visitors, and television for an hour each weekday evening, giving the message that this is quiet time or homework time. Obviously this won't force Tommy to study—that is his responsibility. In addition to limiting the distractions, Tina may require that a school progress report be brought home each Friday. If there are missing assignments or no progress report, Tommy will not be allowed weekend privileges. Parental agreement will reinforce this plan.

Critique the Plan

Does her new response meet the criteria for success?

Is it different from the repeated response? Tina is not yelling or wringing her hands. She has taken a course of action that is different from what she has been doing.

Is it consistent with the underlying goal? Tina is doing something consistent with her specific goal of Tommy improving his grades.

Is it clear? It is clear what she wants from Tommy: no calls, visitors, or television for an hour an evening, and a progress report each Friday with no missing assignments. The consequences, both positive and negative, are also clear. Tina has done a good job of presenting the rules.

Is it doable without assistance from others? She can exercise her response regardless of what Tommy does. If he doesn't do his part, she can respond by sending visitors away, hanging up the phone, and limiting his weekend privileges. If he does well, she can react positively and grant his privileges.

Is it accurate in assignment of responsibility? The monkey is on Tommy's back. He can turn in his assignments and get a progress report, or deal with the consequences. Tina is doing her part presenting, monitoring, and enforcing the rules, and allowing Tommy to do his part.

Tina's recycled response meets the criteria. It may or may not cause Tommy to change his behavior—only Tommy can do that.

Brainstorm Possible Reactions

Because it is highly unlikely that Tommy is going to be pleased with the new response, Tina must anticipate his reaction as much as possible. If angry, what is he likely to do? Tommy may choose to do the following:

Not do an assignment to see if Tina will really restrict his privileges
Ignore the expectations and the restrictions
Cheat on his assignments to get them done
Not bring home a progress report on Friday
Misplace the report
Lie about obtaining the report—he got it but lost it
Forge a progress report, or parts of it
Throw a temper tantrum and punch a hole in the wall

Threaten to hurt himself, or his parents, if he isn't allowed
   to go out
Run away from home

Build Safety Net/Support

If Tommy chooses any one of these options, it is important for Tina to have a plan for responding to each of his possible actions. There are generally four categories of responses on the part of the adolescent: compliance, pushing or testing the limits, avoidance, physical or verbal threats to hurt others or himself.

Compliance. Clearly this would be an acceptable choice! Tina must be sure to follow through on the positives or rewards associated with proper behavior. Sarcastic comments or words concerning her power or her being victorious would be extremely counterproductive.

There is no reason for a child to change his behavior if there are no real consequences to face.

Pushing or testing the limits. Some of Tommy's possible responses are specifically designed to test whether Tina will really follow through on her stated rules, expectations, and consequences. There is no reason for him to change his behavior if there are no real consequences to face. The only way Tommy will know there are consequences is to break the rule. In some strange way, breaking the rule one more time is his first step toward change. He must have a reason—negative consequences—to change before changing makes sense. So if Tina doesn't follow through, nothing will change. Are the consequences for breaking the rule clear, reasonable, and immediately available? She must know the consequences available to her, and how she is going to enforce them.

Avoidance. Running away and withdrawing emotionally are threats usually used to increase noncompliance. Tommy may indeed need some time away from Tina. To keep him from running away, Tina and Larry may need to prearrange an acceptable place for him to be. Another family in her church, relatives, a local youth facility, or a temporary foster home may provide the space she and Tommy both need to cool down. If none of these is available, Tommy's room can be used as a time out room. He must agree to stay there, and Tina must agree not to bother him for the specified period. If he refuses these options and is bent on running away, she may

Stick like glue to him so if he runs she runs after him
Call the police when he runs
Allow him to go
Tell him that she is going to clean his room when he's gone (this is a manipulative ploy because she knows how he'd resent that)
Gather up all of his shoes—it's difficult to run very far in his socks

Physical or verbal threats to hurt others or himself. Some of Tommy's responses are attempts to force the monkey back to Tina. If she gives in to his threats, he will continue to use them. If he threatens suicide or actually does something to hurt himself, she must have an immediate plan available to her. Responses that are usually appropriate are

Dial 911 for immediate medical assistance
Contact pastor, counselor, suicide prevention hot line
Stay with him and don't let him out of her sight
Hospitalize him to insure his safety
Remove any lethal means for hurting himself (pills, guns, knives)
Call others she knows are available to come and provide assistance

Follow through on her plan of police involvement, including pressing charges

Follow through on her commitment to counseling

Questions to Consider

1. If needed, who could you call for support and backup?
2. If your child leaves the house without permission, how will you respond?
3. If your child threatens self-injury, what options do you have to insure his safety?
4. Are the police willing to be involved? To what degree?
5. Is your pastor, church, or local youth counseling agency available to help? In what capacity?

Plan to Limit the Old Response

Parent-child ruts are not always obvious, yet they lurk beneath the surface ready for you to enact, given the right circumstances or cues. Family members become adept at watching for certain cues that set the pattern in motion. Over time, the cues are attended to subconsciously. So if you are going to change your pattern, be aware of the environmental and emotional cues that prompt you to enact a particular pattern. You can then consciously choose to practice your new response, which of course limits the old response.

Environmental Cues

We attend to the environmental stimuli that are important to us and ignore the rest. The water running through the toilet reservoir, the squeaky door, and the clanking furnace motor belt are all cues that prompt my Fixer role. People's faces, their body language, and the tone of their voices are cues I regularly attend to because of my role as a psychologist.

Let's review a typical afternoon to see the environmental cues that trigger Tina's typical responses.

Environmental Cue	Repeated Response	Recycled Response
Tina looks out the kitchen window and sees Tommy walking home without any books in his hands.	Seeing him empty-handed makes her angry. He isn't bringing books home when she knows he isn't passing his classes. When he steps into the house she's ready to ask, "Why didn't you bring home any books?"	Instead of focusing on his hands, she could look at his face. She could then say, "From looking at your face it appears that you had a good (lousy, tiring) day at school. What happened?"
He walks into the house, turns on the television, and plops down for two hours.	Seeing him sit there and waste two hours aggravates her. She comments, "You could have accomplished a lot of work if you'd been studying." She then angrily leaves.	Knowing that he is held captive by television for a while, she could change this interaction by being in the same room and doing something productive—perhaps ironing. Her presence may either allow some positive interaction or non-verbally encourage him to limit his T.V. time.
After television he says that he is bored and wants to do something.	She can't believe that he said that. She would like to tell him, "If you'd do your homework you'd have something to do."	Needing to stay away from the homework issue, she could say, "If you are really that bored, I could sure use some help with my chores."

Environmental Cue	Repeated Response	Recycled Response
He asks if he can go do something fun with a friend.	Still mad about the lack of focus on school work and the tremendous time he wastes, Tina isn't about to let him go see a friend—especially on a school night. So she emphatically states, "You're not going anywhere tonight!"	She could say, "Why don't you invite Don (who is in his algebra class) over to review your algebra. There is soda in the refrigerator that you two could have."

Some of you may be thinking these recycled responses are quite stupid because they did nothing to get him to study. Indeed they didn't. But don't forget that Tina's response of nagging Tommy hasn't worked. Doing more of it won't work either. Stopping the nagging removes at least one of the reasons he isn't doing his work. "The more Mom nags me about doing my homework, the longer I'm going to put it off." Discontinuing the nagging also increases the possibility that their relationship will begin to improve. As long as the relationship is negative, Tommy remains motivated only to irritate Tina. If she moves from anger with his behavior to interest in him, it will improve the quality of their relationship.

What environmental cues prompt your repeated responses? How else could you respond to those cues?

Emotional Cues

Emotional cues such as feeling scared, unsure of yourself, angry, or intimidated can elicit a pattern response. At times, an observer might wonder why the person enacted the pattern as there were no overt cues. The person may have experienced a feeling or emotion, perhaps brought on by a memory, that prompted the pattern behavior. This is particularly true when there is a buildup of emotion. In this situation, even an insignificant cue can trigger a strong repeated response. Understandably, Cain was angry when his offering was not accepted. It certainly seems that Cain experienced a buildup of emotion, as this incident alone doesn't seem enough to prompt the killing of his brother.

Let's review several emotions that Tina might feel concerning Tommy and his homework, and consider possible responses.

Emotion	Repeated Response	Recycled Response
Anger at his lack of dedication to his school work	She angrily asks, "Why won't you try harder in school? You won't get anywhere in life without more commitment."	Rather than blaming, she might express curiosity: "I wonder what interferes with your really doing well in school. Have you ever thought about that?"
Disgust at his lazy lifestyle	She angrily states, "You are the laziest kid I know. Why can't you exert a little more energy?"	Focusing on the positive she could say, "You are a very creative kid. With some focused energy you could really accomplish a lot."
Disappointment in how he wastes his natural abilities	She continually points out how he is wasting his ability: "You don't even use 30 percent of your brain. It's a shame all that intelligence was wasted on you."	"You really are a smart kid." Perhaps adding, "I'm looking forward to seeing you excel when you put that brainpower to use."

Emotion	Repeated Response	Recycled Response
Embarrassment when she receives notices from school concerning his failing grades	Wanting to lay a guilt trip, she says, "Do you know how embarrassing it is to receive these notices? None of my friends' children have ever received them."	Simply wanting to communicate her feelings, Tina could say, "I know these notes don't bother you, but they do embarrass me. I know they shouldn't, but they do."

The negative comments can fuel more resistance, causing a good plan to fail. Granted, the recycled responses by themselves won't change the situation and make Tommmy do his work, but when they are coupled with a well thought out plan it is more likely that progress will occur.

What emotional cues prompt your repeated responses? How could you respond differently to those cues?

Questions to Consider

1. Which of your children do you most often respond to in a negative fashion?
2. What specific behavior from your child triggers your negative response?
3. What environmental cues prompt your spouse and others in your family to enact their parts of the pattern?
4. What emotions trigger your responses, and those of other family members?
5. How could you change or eliminate the cues that prompt negative patterns? (Sometimes changing structure is helpful, such as schedules, routines, order.)

Expect Reaction

People won't like your changes. They are used to you behaving in a certain predictable way. They will pressure you to return to your old response, which is predictable. That may sound silly, especially if the changes are positive, but please remember the Prodigal Son's older brother. Was he happy when the younger brother came to his senses and returned home? No, we see in Luke 15:28 (AMP) that he "was angry, with deep-seated wrath, and resolved not to go in." Someone will be upset with your changes. Count on it.

Recycling your response will make situations and feelings more intense. A departure from what you know well creates new anxiety for you and for others.

You will feel clumsy in trying out your new behavior. The recycled response is strange and unfamiliar, whereas the old was comfortable. As a result it will be tempting to fall back into your rut to avoid anxiety and embarrassment.

Performing a new pattern requires more energy and more self-monitoring. The repeated response was done with very little conscious thought, but the recycled response demands more self-observation.

Environmental and emotional cues will still trigger your old reactions. Because you are not consciously aware of all of them, the task then is to recognize the many cues and consciously enact your recycled response instead of the old one. Doing this requires good observation skills, energy, and persistence.

You will feel discouraged or dumb when you fall back into your old behavior. The unrealistic expectation is that once you are aware of the parent-child rut, you should be able to promptly change it.

You may feel like giving up. You decide that change is not worth it. You are not doing as well as you thought, and no one is appreciating your effort.

God will support efforts consistent with biblical guidelines. He has promised to be with us and help us change (Heb. 13:5;

Phil. 1:6). Look for changes in circumstances that may allow behavior changes to be made more easily!

Set a Date to Evaluate the Plan

It is so easy to go from day to day and not really think about what is going on. Denial is very effective. What makes us complete an assignment, project, letter, or chore? For many of us it is the deadline, the time we are going to be held accountable.

Short time frames are good, especially at the beginning stages of developing a plan. This is how Daniel dealt with not wanting to defile himself by eating the king's food and drinking his wine. In Daniel 1:8–17 we see that the commander wasn't in favor of making any changes concerning Daniel's diet. The commander had much to lose if Daniel's plan failed! Daniel dealt with the situation by offering an alternative, testing it for a brief period of time, and then evaluating the results.

> The commander of the officials said to Daniel, "I am afraid of my lord the king, who has appointed your food and your drink; for why should he see your faces looking more haggard than the youths who are your own age? Then you would make me forfeit my head to the king." . . . "Please test your servants for ten days, and let us be given some vegetables to eat and water to drink. Then let our appearance be observed in your presence, and the appearance of the youths who are eating the king's choice food; and deal with your servants according to what you see."
>
> Daniel 1:10, 12–13

The plan worked, allowing Daniel and his friends to continue eating what they believed to be proper. So try a plan for a week, and at the end of the week sit down and review the pluses and minuses.

Questions to Consider

1. What is one part of the rut you want to change (it doesn't need to be major)? Determine within yourself to make that change. Small changes made by one person can be enough to initiate major changes in a family pattern.
2. What are the personal needs you meet through the enactment of your old pattern? What other ways can you find to meet those needs?
3. What environmental and emotional cues trigger you to enact your old behavior? The more cues you can identify, the more control you will gain.
4. What new environmental cues can you use to trigger your recycled response? The more cues you discover, the sooner the new behavior will become a habit.
5. Who have you enlisted in your support system? Let a few close friends know what you are trying to do so they can support you, encourage you, and pray for you.

Be as consistent with the recycled response as you can be. Remember, a new habit takes time to build. If you only make one big push, people won't believe you are serious and they will wait for you to return to your old ways. They need to see your commitment to the new response before they will begin to adapt to the change in you.

Be supportive of yourself. Reward yourself in some way. Who likes to keep making the effort without seeing any benefit? Cut yourself some slack. Take on a practice mentality: You don't have to do the new behavior perfectly. Remember this is practice, not performance or perfection!

Count on God providing a way to avoid old patterns (1 Cor. 10:13). Look for and use the ways he provides to avoid the old behavior. Don't give up. You *can* do it!

5

How Am I Doing?

Step 4: Evaluate and Modify the Plan

You have identified some of your patterns, have seen which responsibilities belong to whom, and have developed a plan that you want to try for a week. But first, let's set up a way to evaluate how well the plan works.

Direction

When you evaluate the plan a week or so from now, first you must determine if you were headed in the right direction. If you took steps but were facing the wrong direction, you moved away from your goal. This may seem like a given, but facing the right direction is a significant first step and can be a point of encouragement for you. Perhaps you haven't made great strides yet, but heading in the right direction is in fact progress!

Paying attention to direction also provides a way to begin reinforcing a change in your child. For Tommy and his grades, this may be bringing his books home, regardless of whether he actually uses them. Parents may react sarcastically to this change of direction, minimize its importance, or miss it altogether. Tina might say, "Well, it's about time you actually brought a book home. Are you sick?" Comments like these aren't productive for either party. It is better to say nothing than to be negative when your child begins to do what you want. And if you aren't sensitive to the direction he or she is facing, you may miss positive cues you want to reinforce.

Perhaps you haven't made great strides yet, but heading in the right direction is in fact progress!

The Prodigal Son's father is a good model of a parent who could easily have allowed his disappointment to close a chapter of his life. He could have missed the cues of his child's recycled response. But he was ready and watching when his wayward son finally came to his senses and started for home. (Reality can be quite effective in modifying behavior!) "But while he was still a long way off, his father saw him, and felt compassion for him, and ran and embraced him, and kissed him" (Luke 15:20). When he saw his son from a distance—but heading in the right direction—he went to him, embraced him, and encouraged him to return. Note that the father did not rescue him. He didn't go to the far country and beg him to come home. He watched and hoped that his son would come to his senses and return. Incidentally, we also see from Luke 15:31 that the father didn't redivide the inheritance and give the Prodigal Son another share.

Even when it is difficult, keep watching and hoping. This might just be the time your child will make positive changes. Tina's job isn't to make Tommy change, but to notice when he does.

Expectations

Often we think only of how far we are from the expectations. Where you focus determines to a large degree how you feel and how you respond.

You started here	This is where you are now	This is where you want to be
A	B	C

If while standing at point B you

- Look at the distance from B to A, you feel good about the progress you've made, you feel proud of your accomplishment. If you focus on the progress your children have made, you probably say to them, "Good job on the progress! You're doing better."
- Focus exclusively on the distance from B to C, you feel discouraged about how far there is yet to go, and you may be tempted to quit. If you focus on how far your children have to go, you likely say to them, "Hurry up, can't you see how much there is to do without me telling you? For once I would like to see you do something on your own. Get to work."

Because the distance between B and C is often greater than the distance between A and B, there is a natural inclination to focus on the perceived failure to meet a goal rather than on the positive movement you have made (real success).

George MacDonald understood this important distinction concerning God's expectations of us. Certainly our efforts please God, even though he is ultimately satisfied only with perfection (a goal that won't be completed until heaven).

"What father is not pleased with the first tottering attempt of his little one to walk? [But] what father would be satisfied with anything but the manly step of the full-grown son?"*

---

*George MacDonald: An Anthology, ed. C. S. Lewis (London: Geoffrey Bles, 1986), 41.

Concerning this issue, the child usually stresses the progress while the parent emphasizes the distance yet to go. When this occurs, the child doesn't feel like his effort and progress were appropriately recognized and resists exerting any more effort. The parent doesn't feel his concerns were taken seriously and tries to emphasize that point.

	Feels	**Acts**
Child	unappreciated angry resentful	rebellious resistant to expend any more energy stages a sit-down strike
Parent	unheard concerned angry	lectures further emphasizes the goal pushes for more effort and work

Often both parent and child angrily leave this unproductive conversation. This can be avoided by taking time *first* to be genuinely pleased with the effort and progress that has been made. When this has received adequate attention, a parent can then legitimately move on to the distance yet to be traveled

Don't let the distance to go prevent you from feeling good about the progress you have made.

toward the goal. So don't let the distance to go prevent you from feeling good about the progress you have made. Give yourself a pat on the back when you've earned it. Focus on the positive. It really can do wonders for both you and your child.

Evaluation

A plan is a tool to help you accomplish your goal. If it is helpful, it is a good plan. If it doesn't help, a better plan needs to be found. Tina developed a plan concerning Tommy's schoolwork, but before we begin to evaluate it, let's look at what Tommy did for the week.

He didn't bring any books home all week. This was particularly a problem on Wednesday because he had a math midterm on Thursday. He forgot about the school progress report on Friday so he didn't have it to show to his mother. When she pulled his weekend privileges he became so angry that he punched a hole in his bedroom wall. Even though Larry was unhappy about the hole in the wall, he allowed Tommy to go to a party (without his car) on Saturday night.

It would be easy to say that whatever plan Tina had, it obviously didn't succeed. But it is important to remember that you can only change your own behavior. If you exercised your new response and you felt good about it, that is success. Typically we evaluate a plan based on whether it had the exact long-term effect we were looking for. We often want to jump from where we are to where we want to be in one quick movement. Unfortunately it doesn't work that way. It took a while to get into the problem, and it may take some time to get out. Nevertheless, the question still remains, Was Tina's plan a success? The plan was to modify her behavior, so let's look at how she did for the week. The chart on the next page shows the specific behaviors she planned to practice and those she would try to limit. An X in the box means the behavior was present. A blank box means the behavior wasn't present. *NA* means not applicable.

We can see that Tina limited his homework distractions from 7 to 8 P.M., looked to see if he brought books home (change of direction), asked him for the report, and pulled his weekend privileges. She stopped nagging about the homework, except on Wednesday, and reminded him about the school report only once too often. True, the major goal of Tommy turning in more homework wasn't accomplished this week. But several things were accomplished:

Practice New Response	SUN	MON	TUES	WED	THU	FRI	SAT
Limit phone calls from 7–8 P.M.	X	X	X	X	X	NA	NA
Limit visitors from 7–8 P.M.	X	X	X	X	X	NA	NA
Look to see if he brought a book home with plan to positively reinforce	NA	X	X	X	X	X	NA
Ask for school report Friday after school	NA	NA	NA	NA	NA	X	NA
Give or restrict weekend privileges based on compliance	X	NA	NA	NA	NA	X	

Limit Old Response	SUN	MON	TUES	WED	THU	FRI	SAT
Nag about homework				X			
Ask to see completed homework				X			
Remind about school progress report				X		X	

1. Tina began to give Tommy a clear message that the homework was his responsibility, placing the monkey on his back.
2. Tina's frustration about needing to make something happen, with no power to do so, was lessened. Her focus was not on the homework, but on modifying her response. She had power to do that and she did it!
3. She reduced the amount of nagging and yelling at Tommy, thereby reducing her guilt.
4. Tommy and Larry liked less yelling from Tina.

As you can see, Tina didn't do her part perfectly. Even though she tried not to, she did yell at Tommy on Wednesday. The fact that he forgot to bring his math book home before the midterm exam pushed her over the edge. However, she recovered and didn't fall into the same old responses on Thursday, Friday, or Saturday. She continued to look for a positive change of direction.

She thought she was moving along quite nicely by pulling Tommy's weekend privileges. He didn't bring home the progress report and he received the stated consequence. But she was furious at Larry for allowing Tommy to go to the party, and she didn't appreciate Tommy's smug look when he left. In the fight that ensued Larry said the pulling of all his weekend privileges was too harsh, so he allowed Tommy to go to the party but didn't permit him to take his car. Tina didn't think that was much of a punishment because his friends picked him up and they had a great time.

Modification

Even though Tina felt very strongly that pulling all of Tommy's weekend privileges was the only thing that would faze Tommy, Larry wouldn't support it. After considerable discussion, they agreed to allow Tommy only one night out, without his car, if he didn't bring home a satisfactory progress report on Friday. This modification was reported to Tommy. Even though he disliked it, he didn't complain. This was lighter than what he was originally given, and he knew Dad wasn't going to budge.

The following week was basically a repeat of the previous week. Tina continued to do well with not nagging and limiting the interruptions to his quiet/study time. Tommy brought home no books and read *Sports Illustrated* during the study hour. The parents talked about the weekend restrictions and allowed Tommy to go out on Saturday only, without his car. Tommy seemed relatively happy with that. He brought no schoolwork home on Monday, Tuesday, or Wednesday. Formerly this would have caused Tina to yell because Tommy wasn't taking more responsibility for his grades. Interestingly, because Tina wasn't nagging and yelling, Larry's usual response of calming her down wasn't required and his focus shifted from Tina to Tommy's lack of cooperation and effort. Thursday morning at the breakfast table he talked with Tina about his concern and together they decided they needed to be firmer with Tommy. As Tommy was walking out the door, Larry told him that he would have no weekend privileges unless he had a satisfactory progress report on Friday. Tommy responded with "Well, fine! I can't have that by Friday, so there is no use in going to school today." He then slammed the door and left.

It took three more weeks with no weekend privileges before Tommy brought home a progress report. When he brought the report home, his parents allowed him to go out one night without his car. The following week's progress report reflected improvement in all of his classes and only one unsatisfactory grade. The tension in the house continued to decrease as Tommy's grades improved. Tina's guilt diminished and she felt better about Tommy and his grades, allowing her to be more positive with him.

Practice

Making a similar chart (see the sample on the next page), list your behavioral goals. This will help keep you account-able for those responsibilities that are legitimately yours.

Clearly there is a connection between success and effort. A good plan is worth investment of energy. If you think it is a good plan but didn't really follow it, try it for another week.

Questions to Consider

Direction

1. Did the plan help you to face the right direction?
2. Did it give you a way to modify your usual pattern?
3. Did the plan help you to keep looking for positive changes?
4. Did you refrain from sarcastic comments when your child turned in the right direction?
5. Were you able to keep going after you hit a snag, or felt like you failed?

Expectations

1. Did your plan help you stay focused on the positive movement, and not just on how far you have to go?
2. Regardless of how it worked, did you give your-self a pat on the back for trying?
3. Were you able to reinforce any positive move-ment by your child?
4. Did dissatisfaction keep you from being pleased with *some* progress?
5. How did you feel when you tried your new response?

(continued on page 87)

Practice New Response	SUN	MON	TUES	WED	THU	FRI	SAT

Limit Old Response	SUN	MON	TUES	WED	THU	FRI	SAT

Evaluation

1. Did the plan help you to be more accountable for your behavior?
2. Did the plan help you to hold your child more accountable for his or her behavior?
3. Was the plan easy to follow?
4. Did the plan help motivate you?
5. What changes could be made to improve the plan?

Effort

1. On a scale from 1 to 10 (with 1 being *no effort expended* and 10 being *really worked hard*) how hard did you actually work on the plan?
2. On a scale from 1 to 10 (with 1 being *no success* and 10 being *great success*) how successful was the plan?

PART 2

Getting Out of Those Ruts

Changing is not easy.

It takes a lot of hard work.

But you can do it and

it's worth it.

6

Why Can't You See It My Way?

Rut 1: Parental Disagreement

It was certainly a match made in heaven. Abraham gave clear, strict instructions to his servant for finding Isaac a bride. The servant's compliance with those instructions, coupled with his request for God's divine direction, yielded a beautiful virgin named Rebekah. There was no doubt she was the wife for Isaac (Gen. 24). But this perfect match turned into a heated match through the years. Instead of working together they took sides with their children: Isaac with Esau and Rebekah with Jacob.

When Rebekah protected Jacob and conned Isaac into sending him to be with her brother Laban in a neighboring country (Gen. 27:43–28:7), it showed that the husband-wife relationship had undoubtedly been strained. This had limited their parental effectiveness and created fierce conflict between their sons. What started as a perfect match

Isaac	Rebekah
Isaac loved Esau because he had a taste for game (Gen. 25:28)	*But* Rebekah loved Jacob (Gen. 25:28)
Isaac wanted to bless Esau (27:1–4)	*But* Rebekah wanted Jacob to receive the blessing (27:6–10)
Isaac sent Esau to hunt for meat so they could eat (27:3–4)	*But* Rebekah sent Jacob to bring two choice goats so he and Isaac could eat (27:8–10)
Isaac meant to bless Esau and thought he accomplished that (27:24–29)	*But* Rebekah meant for Isaac to bless Jacob and saw that accomplished (27:27–30)

ended by the family being torn apart because of the lack of parental unity.

Step 1: Recognize Parental Disagreement

As we have seen with Isaac and Rebekah, the parents in this rut are not in agreement. This allows the child to manipulate to get more of what he or she wants. If this occurs in your family, the following situations may be seen.

Is This the Picture in Your Home?

Your child works the two of you against each other. Your daughter asks permission from the parent who is more likely to give her the answer she wants. She then goes to the other parent and says, "Mom said that it was okay with her if it's okay with you." In some cases, she may not even have checked with the other parent, simply reporting that Mom or Dad "said it was okay." If you don't like what she's requesting, you are set up to be angry with your spouse because he or she already gave permission.

There is increasing tension between you and your spouse over disagreements concerning discipline, privileges, chores, and expectations. The parental argument tends to focus on which parent is right, and ironically each parent usually has a valid point of view. Moms generally are concerned about the child's feelings, while dads usually are more concerned about the child's meeting some standard of performance. Together they would actually have a comprehensive, balanced approach.

If the tension is high enough, it can dissolve a marriage.

You certainly are aware of the tension between you and your spouse but you may not have noticed that it centers on parenting issues. Mentally remove the parenting conflicts and see how much conflict remains. If the tension is high enough, it can dissolve a marriage.

The monkey resides on a parent's back. You or your spouse carry additional responsibility that legitimately belongs to your child—you do the trash, dishes, or cleaning because it is easier than hassling your child to get it done. Or the child can avoid responsibility because the rules are not presented, monitored, and enforced clearly and consistently.

Your child heeds only what she wants to hear. Your adolescent picks out parts of parental conversations and uses them to personal advantage. She chooses the parent's view that she likes the most and follows that directive. It is hard to punish her because one parent was obeyed. That leaves Mom and Dad upset with each other, which creates further problems in reaching agreement.

Your child experiences repeated consequences for noncompliance with rules at school, at work, and in the community. When parents haven't consistently enforced their rules, the child learns over time that she can ignore them. Eventually she thinks society's rules are for everyone else but her! Thus, she faces more and more consequences.

Sibling conflict is increasing. The children see the parental unfairness and complain about it. When parents don't take care of it, the children, out of anger and resentment, increase their fighting to get their fair share.

Repeated Responses in Parental Disagreement

It is easy to focus on one response and then get stuck there. Here are some unproductive repeated responses parents often use in an attempt to move past their parental disagreement.

Try to convince your spouse you are right so you can win the argument. You believe that things would be wonderful if you could just get him to see the light. If you came up with just the right evidence, or clearly pointed out the flaws in his logic, he would be convinced and would agree with you. The two of you could then deal appropriately with your child. Unfortunately, the focus is to delete one point of view rather than to blend your perspectives.

Enlist power or support from others to force your spouse to concede to your point of view. Enlistees often include children, extended-family members, pastors ("spiritual" power may help), authors (through their books), and counselors. Involving more people in the parental arena generally makes agreement harder to reach, unless both parents agree to seek help.

Strongly enforce your rules and don't enforce your spouse's rules. Some parents specifically tell the child to disobey the other parent's rules, while others passively undermine the rules of their spouse by simply not enforcing them. This teaches your child that obedience is based on who is present, rather than on the correctness or helpfulness of the rule. This shows your child that you don't respect your spouse's opinion, so why should she? Don't be surprised when this principle is used against you, by the way.

Enforce few rules, or none at all. Usually, the lenient parent is viewed by the child as being more reasonable and likable. This further undermines the parents' unity.

Punish your spouse, directly or indirectly, until he or she agrees with you. Clearly this increases the conflict in the marital relationship. Punishment can include not coming home, spending money, abuse, drinking, withholding sex, having an affair.

Did any of this sound familiar? Think about the following factors that may keep you locked into one of these repeated responses in parental disagreements.

- Consider your beliefs. Your different beliefs may be the reason the two of you cannot reach agreement. Isaac believed that Esau should receive the blessing as the first-born. Rebekah probably believed that Jacob should receive the blessing based on the prophecy that the older brother would serve the younger one (Gen. 25:22–24). Clearly Isaac and Rebekah weren't in agreement. Instead of dealing with those differing beliefs, each pursued an agenda of promoting his or her favored son.
- Understand your underlying motivation. What do you really want to accomplish in this disagreement with your spouse? Are you wanting to get your way? What do you think would happen if you did things your spouse's way? Trying one way for a specified period would move you beyond impasse.
- Examine your parents' example. You may have grown up with a model of parental disunity. If that is the case, you know exactly how to behave when you don't agree with your spouse. If your parents didn't present a united front, and if you married someone with whom agreement is very difficult, you may take total control of a situation or you may abdicate all responsibility.
- Study your role(s). You may be a Protector married to an Enforcer, for example. Because the behavior and goals of these roles are incompatible, you and your spouse will have trouble reaching agreement. Do your roles blend together to create a balance, or do they conflict to the point where one must win the right to dictate the rules?

- Check your relationships. You may be on the side of the child who is at odds with your spouse. Taking sides will make it harder to reach agreement with your mate.

Step 2: Clarify Responsibility

Present Expectations

If the speed limit sign had both 40 and 65 on it, which speed would you drive? Similarly if you and your spouse aren't in agreement, your child can choose which parental expectation to meet. By not being in agreement, you leave a loophole that most children will use.

Monitor Compliance

Without this agreement, your child's behavior could be considered both acceptable and unacceptable. She can't be expected to comply when the expectations are unclear.

Enforce Consequences

If your child obeys one of the parental directives, she can make a good case for saying she obeyed and therefore shouldn't be punished.

Step 3: Make a Plan to Change Your Response

This rut won't release you by itself. The child will continue to work one parent against the other to gain what she wants, and the tension in the marriage continues to build.

It is difficult to hold your child
accountable if you provided the loophole.

The child will eventually behave in the outside world in the same way she does at home. The rules are not really meant for her. She doesn't intend to follow them since her experience indicates that there are no consequences to pay, plus the rules will probably change anyway. Thus the child continues to disregard rules, and the world begins to impose harsher penalties for bad behavior.

Determine the Goal

To break out of this particular rut, there are two major goals to achieve. First, you must reach parental unity so you can give your child a clear message of what you expect. Until parents have worked out a compromise or a way of dealing with the situation, it is almost impossible to hold your child accountable for her behavior. Second, return the monkey to your child so she can begin to modify her behavior to bring it into line with your expectations. It would be great if reaching agreement with your husband or wife meant that your child would automatically follow your rules. Unfortunately, she must learn that you are in agreement, and that you will follow through on the consequences. Typically she learns this by breaking the rule and seeing that you meant what you said. (During this time you will have more opportunity to work on parental unity!)

Reaching agreement allows the parents to change their response, thus facilitating a change in the child's behavior. (See chart on the following page.)

Develop a Plan

Parents must be in a position where they are emotionally ready and willing to work together. A number of things can interfere with working on a realistic plan.

Too much negative marital history will prevent a couple from negotiating their parenting differences. Resolving these old wounds involves talking about them and forgiving them. A referral to marital therapy can be a prerequisite to family therapy.

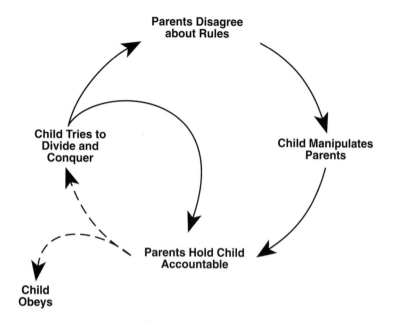

Denying that there is a problem or pretending it is okay doesn't move you one step toward a solution. Difficulty is created by denial of the needs, or trying to minimize their importance, essentially stating verbally or nonverbally:

"It's okay."
"It doesn't really bother me that much."
"It's only a stage."
"He's so busy this time of the year that I don't want to bother him with my needs."
"Given time, it will change."

It will aggravate the situation to avoid the spouse and look to God to meet the needs. Certainly there are some needs that only God can meet, and to expect other humans to meet those needs will always result in disappointment. But escaping to God in order to avoid problems with your spouse will not help you—or please God.

To work through your differences you will need to learn to compromise and to make decisions together.

Denying that there is a problem or pretending it is okay doesn't move you one step toward a solution.

Agree! Compromise!

Reach a mutually agreed upon position or plan concerning your child. If you are stuck, try one of the following suggestions.

Pay attention to the pattern of your fights. Parents typically use the same argument strategies over and over. Changing part of the pattern can change the outcome. So what is the pattern when you disagree with your spouse? You might try tape-recording one of your discussions so you can listen to it at a later point. This may help you to change the pattern in some way: timing, sequencing, place, and so forth.

The Pattern	The Change
Instead of focusing on the negative	*Focus on the positive—identify what is working and do more of it*
Talk	Write
Do it live	Tape your side for your spouse
Monopolize	Say what you think in one sentence
Ramble	Talk for only 2 minutes at a time (use a timer)
Avoid	Hold hands and look at each other
Argue at home	Discuss at a restaurant
Yell	Whisper
Face each other	Sit back-to-back on the floor

Seek input to reach a balanced solution. In some relationships one spouse, often the wife, communicates considerably more than the other. When there is an absence of input from the nontalker, this not only severely limits the possibilities for problem solving, but also diminishes the balance necessary between

abstract and concrete
practical and principled
conservative and liberal
safe and risky
punishing and forgiving
generosity and stinginess
boring and exciting

In other situations one of the spouses, usually the husband, is the sole authority in the family. The spouse without the power can become resentful and may side with the children against the other's overbearing qualities. Mother may covertly support one of the children for talking back to Dad, telling what the whole family–particularly Mother–wants him to know.

You need input from both sides of the disagreement to reach a balanced, sensible outcome.

Each side needs to understand the other's viewpoints. To help understand, you might swap sides and argue the other view or summarize in your own words your spouse's opinion. Your mate can then tell you how close you are to understanding what he or she said. If winning the argument, rather than increasing understanding, becomes the focus, it is time to take a break.

Set a time when you are both ready to talk about the issues. Arrange a place and a time without interruption or interference from the children, phone, work, or other concerns. Don't talk about the issues when the timing is poor, or when you are tired or pressured. This only creates more anger and discouragement.

Find some common ground. It is quite likely that you both have at least some similar underlying motivation (for example, safety, responsibility, fun, positive relationships). Find that area of agreement and from there see if you can build a plan on which you can agree.

Deal with one issue at a time. Write the issue on a sheet of paper and keep it in front of you. When you stray from the issue, refocus. Don't expect to deal with all of your disagreements at one time. Determine between you the top two or three concerns. Agree to focus on one of them at the present time. Deal with it before moving on to the next issue.

Stay solution-focused. Try to come up with solutions rather than falling back on blaming, faultfinding, or name calling. If you can't agree on how much freedom your daughter should have because of her poor attitude and bad grades, don't worry about general guidelines. Instead, focus on what privileges you can both agree on that she should have for tomorrow. When tomorrow is settled, work on the next day. That will at least get you moving in a positive direction with a clear message to your daughter.

Make Decisions Together

Don't allow your child to divide and conquer. Agree with your spouse that decisions will be made together and then presented to your child. Most decisions can be postponed until you and your spouse get together and privately discuss what should be done. This will limit the child's ability to cause dissension. If she can't wait until the two of you have time to discuss the issue, then answer with no.

Practice

Use the following chart to practice your new responses and limit your old ones. Put an *X* in the corresponding days

Parental Behaviors

Date to Evaluate: _____

Practice New Response	SUN	MON	TUES	WED	THU	FRI	SAT
Followed the agreed upon plan							
Solicited and used input from both parents							
Took time to privately discuss problems before giving answers							
Reviewed the expectations and consequences with our child							
Followed through on positive and negative consequences							

Limit Old Response	SUN	MON	TUES	WED	THU	FRI	SAT
Disagreed with spouse in front of child							
Enforced only my rules							
Undermined spouse							
Punished spouse because he or she disagreed with me							

where the behavior is present. The *X*s are desirable in the top chart and undesirable in the bottom one.

Anticipate Your Child's Reaction

When you make changes and parental unity begins to gel, your child will have a definite response.

She may increase her efforts to work the two of you against each other. If the right buttons are pushed, you may revert to your old response of fighting with each other. If she is successful, she won't need to change. Remember that your child must test this newly formed parental agreement to see if it is for real. She won't begin to change her behavior until she is fairly well convinced that you both mean business.

She may look for new areas where the two of you might not agree. She may not hassle you about the new curfew, but she may push on the amount of "grace time" that you grant. Or she may acknowledge that she was a little late but, she says, she deserves only a minor consequence. If you and your spouse don't agree on this consequence, her being "only ten minutes late" may once again divide the two of you.

She may "kiss up" to parents individually. If she can get one of you to shift to her point of view, she doesn't have to worry about the other parent. She may go after the weaker parent, or the one she feels will be more sympathetic to her cause. This occurred with Samson.

This story in the Book of Judges is a mixed bag concerning parental unity, giving us great examples of what to do and what not to do. Samson's mother discussed with her husband, Manoah, the visit of the "man of God" (Judg. 13:6, 10). Good! Parents need to discuss important information about their child.

They were together in their offering to the Lord (v. 19). We are also given a conversation that occurred between the two after they realized that the man was really the "angel of the LORD," an Old Testament manifestation of Jesus Christ.

Manoah was correct theologically when he feared they were going to die because they had seen God (v. 22). His wife was correct practically in that if God meant to kill them, he would not have shown them all that he did (v. 23). This is a beautiful example of how input from both spouses productively deals with a situation. This is how it should work.

Later, we see they both answered Samson about marrying someone from the Israelite community (14:3). Then something very important happened when Samson talked only to his father, attempting to divide and conquer. If this ploy works, he may get his way. Will the parents stick together?

We find both parents going to Timnah, but then his "father went down to the woman" (v. 10). It worked! When Samson spoke only to Dad, Dad succumbed, and Samson got what he wanted. Samson separated his parents, making them unable to follow through on God's directive and on their family rule.

She may completely disregard the rule and the consequences to see if you'll force her to obey. If she chooses this option, you will need to establish consequences that don't require her cooperation. She may choose to go out, but she won't be able to take the family car because you won't give her the keys.

When she begins to understand that you are united, she will see that her energy is best spent in trying to meet your expectations. Only at this point is the monkey transferred to her back, and perhaps she will try new positive coping strategies.

No one said you had to perform the new response perfectly all of the time.

So far you are doing very well. You have a plan, you are working on that plan, and you are finding new cues to prompt your new response. Don't forget that the old response is lurking! Lack of sleep, a lousy day at work, or catching a cold may make it easy for the old response to emerge. Don't despair. This is practice, not perfection. No one said you had to perform the new response perfectly all of the time. It doesn't need to be a big deal if you blow it. See what you can do to recover and move on.

Set a Date to Review the Plan

Having a specific time to review the plan helps keep you accountable. Keep in mind we are evaluating a plan. If the plan doesn't work, it doesn't necessarily mean that you have failed. It may mean that the plan needs to be modified. You may recall Mad Hatter's plan, in *Alice In Wonderland,* to fix the broken watch. He used the very best butter available, but it didn't work. If your plan didn't work, move on. But do review it so you can use the information to develop a better plan.

Step 4: Evaluate and Modify the Plan

Evaluate the Plan

Direction

Did you stay focused on working together? If you realized more quickly that you were giving different messages, you are definitely facing the right direction! Did your child change direction (for example, stop trying to manipulate the two of you)? If so, this is an opportunity to reinforce her behavior. If your child didn't change, did you keep watching for change?

Expectations

Before considering how far you are from your goal, take time to look at what you did to make progress this week. Review the chart you made and see what you did well. What worked, and is there a way to do more of that?

Evaluate Your Behavior and Feelings

1. Did you feel good about your behavior?
2. With which specific goals did you succeed?
3. What did you do to make that progress?
4. Has that changed your level of anger or frustration?
5. What was hard for you?
6. What did your spouse do well?
7. Did you tell him or her?

Evaluate Your Child's Behavior and Feelings

1. Did your plan have any effect on your child?
2. Did your plan appropriately place more of your child's responsibility back on her shoulders?

Modify the Plan

Modifying the plan allows you the opportunity to make changes. You want to do more of what worked, and less of what didn't. The focus then is on removing obstacles or developing a structure that allows you to do more of what worked. In reviewing the chart you may find that talking together privately before giving answers really worked well, but you only did that on Wednesday. Setting up a specific time to review your children's requests may allow you to work together more consistently.

Commit to the Revised Plan

Set a specific date to review the plan again in about a week. This should give you ample time to try the modified plan and determine its viability. When you as parents agree on the expectations and consequences you can realistically hold your child accountable for her behavior.

7

It's My Fault and I Can't Fix It

Rut 2: Parental Guilt

"I just feel so sorry for Jessica. She really misses her father. It would help so much if he would just come by to see her once in a while. He didn't give her a present or even a card for her thirteenth birthday. She was so disappointed. I dread Christmas. Why can't he see how much she misses him? Just a little of his time would mean so much to her. What am I supposed to do?"

It is not surprising that the parent who struggles most often with guilt is the single mom. The issue she feels the most guilty about is the lack of a male role model for her children. The guilt drives her to either overdo for the children—trying to be Supermom—or to be on a continual manhunt. No matter what Mom does, she can't be the dad, and shouldn't try. Furthermore, the children no longer have a father in the home and need to adjust to that loss. Until they come to grips with that loss, they will be unable to accept someone new in the Dad role.

Step 1: Recognize Parental Guilt

Is This the Picture in Your Home?

The striking feature of this rut is that it can happen only with a caring, energetic parent. You may not feel like a good parent, but you wouldn't be caught in this rut if you didn't care, or if you weren't willing to invest energy to make things better for you and your child. Actually your guilt probably results in your being *too nice* to your children! Please understand it isn't my intention to add more things to your to do list, or to the things-you-should-feel-guilty-about list.

There are two parts of parental guilt. First, you have assumed ownership for the problem—you believe it's your

Most parents who feel guilty are caring, energetic people.

fault; second, you have assumed responsibility for fixing it, even though you can't—but you keep trying. You believe you must keep the monkey on your back.

As a result, your guilt alters your response to your child, who is aware of this dynamic and uses the guilt to manipulate you via your emotions. The guilty parent mistakenly believes that if the bad things hadn't occurred, the child would always be happy. So making and keeping your child happy is the only way to avoid the guilt. You as the monkey owner are working very hard to make things smooth for your child. Often this prevents him or her from learning healthier ways of coping.

If this rut occurs in your family, you probably see some of the following.

An overindulged child. Giving him things may make up for the rough or unfortunate situation such as divorce, death of a parent, abandonment by a parent, unfair treatment, physical handicap, or illness. Even though he has everything you can possibly provide, he still isn't happy.

An immature child. Because of your guilt, you have expected very little from your child. When things became somewhat difficult, you smoothed the way and didn't let him struggle much. He has become comfortable being taken care of and hasn't kept up with the maturity rate of others the same age.

A child having difficulty handling privileges. Because of parental guilt, the child has inappropriate privileges for his age. Privileges are given on the basis of parental guilt rather than on the basis of the child's maturity or responsibility level. Your child may have more privileges than he can handle.

A child struggling with relationships. The child is unable to maintain positive relationships, has sexually focused relationships, or dates much older people. The child is in relationships he isn't ready to handle but has the privileges because of parental guilt.

A child in an increasing number of conflicts with those in authority. He is used to being told yes, so when he receives a no he really doesn't know how to handle it. He tries to use guilt, but if that doesn't work, he throws a temper tantrum, creating further problems for himself.

Crises that cause the focus to shift from parental guilt to the child's inappropriate behavior. This shift is the result of two factors: the parent becomes tired of carrying the guilt and struggling with it all the time, and the child's behavior goes over the edge of what the parent is willing to tolerate–the last straw kind of thing.

A parent in an unsatisfactory romantic relationship. Many single parents feel guilty about not having the opposite sex parent figure present in the home. Because they feel that figure is so necessary, they may marry too quickly, settling for less than what they want in a spouse. This creates a tense, undesirable stepfamily situation and even more guilt for themselves. Or a parent may go through one relationship after another in attempts to find a role model for the children.

Repeated Responses in Parental Guilt

Are you stuck in any of the following responses as attempts to manage your guilt?

Give in, to reduce your guilt. Some parents believe they can reduce their own guilt by simply allowing the child to do what he wants to do. This doesn't work. It doesn't reduce guilt, and it doesn't help the child manage his life circumstances.

Avoid thinking about guilt. Avoiding the guilt through denial, busyness, illicit relationships, sex, alcohol, food, or drugs only works temporarily. The guilt continues to exert its influence on your decisions and the parent-child relationship. You may also overlook a situation or avoid a necessary conversation with your child because the topic arouses your guilt.

Try to make up for losses and difficulties. Parents naturally want to counterbalance those negative occurrences that lower the child's quality of life. There are two cautions to observe when trying to make up for bad experiences.

First, does your compensation actually interfere with your child's coping with his unfortunate circumstances? Children need to reach some resolution concerning their predicament. This clearly can be an uncomfortable process for both the child and the parent. A simplistic but clear analogy would be a child who has a stone in his shoe. As his parent, you might do a lot to help him tolerate the discomfort caused by the stone (let him lie on the couch, carry him, drive him places, do errands for him). Doing some or all of these things might make it tolerable to have the stone in his shoe. But really it would be much simpler to have him take off his shoe and dump out the stone. Certainly resolving emotional issues isn't that easy. It takes time, and can be inconvenient. And the difficult part for you is allowing your child to wrestle and struggle with the emotions he feels concerning his circumstances. But if he doesn't do that, he will continue in life with an emotional "stone" in his personality. Use your support and energy to help him face his emotions, not to avoid them.

Second, is what you give him good for him? Parents can give their children things that are fun and enjoyable but not good for them (too much candy, money, toys, material things, freedom). This is overindulgence.

Do all the adjusting and not expect or allow your children to adjust. Children need to confront their misfortune. You must support and encourage them to do so. Your doing all of the adjusting isn't healthy for you or for them.

Blame others. If your spouse left and has no contact with the children, it is easy to focus much anger on him or her. Shifting your focus from blaming to coping is not easy, comfortable, or familiar. Generally, we know how to be angry at someone, but we aren't as sure how to cope—especially if the circumstances are out of our control. So what do you do to shift away from your anger? You must look at your sadness, hurt, disappointment, or helplessness. It really is much easier to blame and be angry, but that doesn't move you toward overcoming your dilemma.

Did any of this sound familiar? Think about the following factors that may keep you locked into one of these guilt responses.

- Consider your beliefs. Parents torn by guilt have many beliefs that need to be discussed and evaluated. Saying the beliefs out loud or writing them down is helpful in being able to really see them and turn loose of them. Typically, parents believe some of the following.

It's all my fault that this happened.
I'm the only one who can fix it.
If I don't fix it, my child will never recover.

If you have made these statements, or thought them, you have assumed complete responsibility for the adversity and for the remedy. This is understandable as you don't want to

Can you trust God to be a part of the answer?

contend with the anxiety created by allowing others to assume control. After all, if you had had complete control to start with, the circumstances probably would not have occurred. Can you allow others to be a part of the solution? Can you trust God to be a part of the answer? What part should your child have in overcoming the situation?

- Understand your underlying motivation. In these cases, the parent is almost always very caring and conscientious and wants very much for things to be better. Parental motivation usually includes a strong desire to accomplish the following:

    Make up for or compensate the child for hardships in his life. The parent feels badly for what has occurred and tries to make life a bit easier for the child. But if Mom buys a birthday gift and signs absent Dad's name to the card, what has she really done for her child? The child at some point must grapple with the fact that he has a dad who doesn't seem to care about him. Because it isn't talked about, many children erroneously believe that there is something wrong with them. They are damaged goods. Otherwise Dad would have stayed, or at least would have stayed in contact with them.

Save the child from additional pain or difficulties. In the case of a single mother, she may try to be both parents by trying to do guy things with her son. *Ease parental guilt.* The parent will do a variety of things to ease guilt. This can take the form of relaxing rules, buying whatever the child wants, or excessive sacrificing.

- Examine your parents' example. How did your parents handle events that were difficult for you? Neither extreme of doing everything for the child or of making the child do everything himself is helpful for parent or child. Based on your parents' example, are you more apt to do too much to ease your child's struggles, or not enough?
- Study your role(s). Does your role make you more susceptible to guilt's negative effects? The following roles are driven by guilt.

    Supermom. This is the most common role that moms assume. They are going to make it by themselves. This is an exhausting role and one that isn't particularly helpful for Mom or the children.
    White Knight. Some men want to ride in with sword flashing and fix everything so the child won't have to ever hurt again. It won't work. You are the only one who can overcome your hurt; only your child can surmount his hurt.

- Check your relationships. Do you feel especially guilty concerning one of your children? If so, is that child apt to receive more compensation from you?

Step 2: Clarify Responsibility

Parental guilt greatly influences the usual presenting expectations, monitoring compliance, and enforcing consequences sequence.

113

Present Expectations

The guilty parent doesn't present many expectations to the child. Furthermore, the child really wouldn't be expected to comply or obey because of the terrible things that have occurred in his life.

Monitor Compliance

The parent closely monitors the child's happiness, not his behavior or his responsibility level. The parent is more concerned with the child's happiness than with holding him accountable for his behavior.

Enforce Consequences

Enforce is a bad word for the guilty parent as it creates an opportunity for the child to clearly restate the terrible deeds of the parent that caused the whole mess. If consequences are enforced, the child is very willing to help the parent feel guilty. Consequences are thus decreased in severity or forgotten altogether.

Step 3: Make a Plan to Change Your Response

Determine the Goal

The chief goal is simply to deal with your guilt so you can hold your children accountable for their behavior. Managing your feelings concerning the situation will give them permission to wrestle with their feelings. When you have yours sorted out, you will then be able to change your repeated response to a recycled response, as indicated on the next page. When you change, you will be assisting them to change.

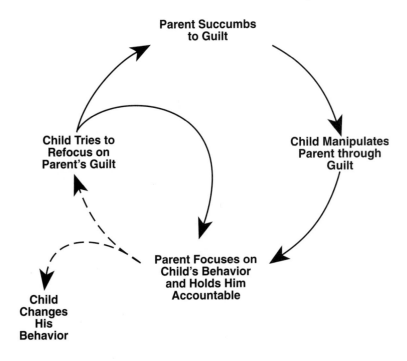

Parent Succumbs
to Guilt

Child Tries to
Refocus on
Parent's Guilt

Child Manipulates
Parent through
Guilt

Child
Changes
His
Behavior

Parent Focuses on
Child's Behavior
and Holds Him
Accountable

Develop a Plan

Deal with Your Guilt

If you are stuck with a lot of guilt, these suggestions may be useful.

Identify the reason you feel guilty.

> "I feel guilty because I dragged my children through many abusive relationships."
>
> "I know it doesn't make sense, but I feel guilty because their dad never sends them anything for Christmas or for their birthdays."
>
> "I feel guilty because I have to work at night when they are home. But if I didn't work that shift, we wouldn't make it."

Identify choices you had at the time of the guilt-producing incident(s). What specific choices did you have available to you? Do you feel guilty for not taking choices that weren't even available to you?

Evaluate the choices that you made. Did you know at the time what you know now about the end result? Usually people make the best decision they could have at the time. Would people you respect likely have done the same thing or made the same decision, given those same circumstances? Ask one of them.

Imagine the changes that would occur if you let go of the guilt.

Who benefits from your feeling guilty?
How would your life be different if you no longer felt guilty?
How would that change your family life or family patterns?

Confess, apologize, and make amends. Doing so should allow you to turn loose your guilt. God certainly is willing to forgive, and others may if you give them a chance (Ps. 32:3–5; 1 John 1:9; Matt. 5:24).

Clarify who is responsible. Be clear on your duties and do them. Take care of the speck in your eye (Matt. 7:3–5). Don't accept responsibility for others' actions. Remember, you can't change something if you don't have control of it. Your energy to change a spouse or force him or her to have contact with your child is wasted energy. God will hold others accountable, so focus your energy on what you can do (Rom. 12:19; Deut. 32:35). Don't accept blame or guilt (or even praise) for your child's responsibilities.

Carefully Assess Your Child's Requests

Is the request really good for him? If you didn't feel guilty, would you allow him to do what he requested? Take the time you need to think about it. Don't give mixed or confusing messages. Let your yes mean yes, and your no mean no.

Don't say no and then after he harasses you change it to yes. Say yes as much as you can.

Be Clear about Consequences

In stepfamilies, the guilty parent often leaves the consequences up to the stepparent to figure out and impose. This usually creates resentment in both the biological parent and the child toward the stepparent because the consequences are viewed as too harsh. Unfortunately this further reinforces the stepparent as the bad guy. State what you believe to be an appropriate consequence and work toward a compromise with your spouse. Then impose that consequence.

Obtain the Needed Help for Your Child

Your actions, or those of others, may have caused problems in the past. Both you and your child can focus on the damage and be miserable for a long time. Rather than looking at the harm, it is much more productive to focus on the solutions. What is needed to move on? Provide that which is needed to press ahead. That may include counseling, finding a big brother or sister to provide a positive relationship and appropriate adult role model, obtaining mental health care, or providing for physical needs such as necessary medication, eye glasses, clothing, or dental work.

Practice

Use the chart on page 118 to practice your new responses and limit your old ones.

Put an *X* in the corresponding days where the behavior was present. The *X*s are desirable in the top chart and undesirable in the bottom one.

Anticipate Your Child's Reaction

If you change your behavior so he can't use your guilt, he will increase his efforts to access your guilt. After all, he has

Parental Behaviors

Practice New Response	SUN	MON	TUES	WED	THU	FRI	SAT
Dealt with my guilt							
Made decisions based on biblical standards and reasonable guidelines rather than guilt							
Followed through on appropriate consequences, positive and negative							
Followed through on a course of action to reduce the negative effects of the unfortunate events							
Supported my child to face his emotions regarding the significant events that caused my guilt							

Limit Old Response	SUN	MON	TUES	WED	THU	FRI	SAT
Accepted the blame for the problem							
Excused his behavior because of the unfortunate circumstances							
Gave in because of guilt							
Did all of the adjusting or accommodating							

learned that the best way to get to you and thus get what he wants is via your guilt.

He may point out new ways that you are responsible for his plight. You will hear him say: "You know Mom, this whole problem started when you divorced Dad. If Dad was here, I wouldn't be doing this poorly in school. Don't you remember that in seventh and eighth grade I had all As and Bs?"

You are now the cause of his low grades! If you believe that or allow him to believe that, you will need to add homework and studying to your already long list of duties! If he has poor study habits, help him learn good habits. If he needs a tutor, provide one for him. But don't accept the responsibility for his grades. Pass the monkey back to him. He is responsible for his studying and his grades.

He may push you to become so angry that you say or do something that you will later regret. Usually this occurs when you say no. He doesn't like that answer and pushes until you become very angry and lose control. Because you feel so badly about overreacting, you give him a yes. You made it successfully past the first opportunity to operate on your guilt by saying no to an unreasonable request, but got snared at the second chance because you felt so badly about how you reacted. It doesn't matter whether you tripped at the first or second scenario: He got what he wanted by using your guilt.

The best thing to do then in these situations is to walk away before you act on your frustration. Some children won't allow a parent to walk away. Your child may follow you everywhere in the house—even to the bathroom (there is nothing fun about having a fight through the bathroom door). You may need to run around the block or even drive away. The key is to not let him push you to the point where you act regrettably and then feel more guilt.

He may tell others that you are responsible for his problems. You are really not excited about having the whole world know that you have failed as a parent. That is one of the reasons you may not want to go to counseling. It would give him an audience to rehearse your shortcomings. If your child thinks that threatening you by broadcasting your faults will cause you to give in, he will threaten. To take the power away from the threat, tell him you will both go to counseling so each of you can have an opportunity to fully explain your point of view.

He may say or hint that he is no longer happy living with you. When you hit this point, you should know that he has pulled out the big guns. This is probably the ultimate in power plays. He says: "I really don't like the way things are going here. I've been thinking that it's time for me to go live with Dad. He and I don't fight, and I think he would treat me better than you do. My grades would go up, and I would be happier. But I suppose you won't let me do that 'cuz then you wouldn't have me for slave labor."

His comments can have a powerful impact on you. Depending on your response, the power in his statements can be enhanced or diffused. You are now in a position to say and do things that could create a tremendous amount of guilt for you. Stop and think. Is he saying this to manipulate you, or because he really wants to live with his father?

If he is using his statement as a threat to get what he wants, don't give it any merit or credence by responding to it. "You aren't going to the show tonight no matter what you threaten.

Don't forget that the old response lurks beneath the surface!

You weren't in on time last weekend so you've lost your privileges this weekend." Walk away.

If he is making the statement because he really does want to go live with his dad, you could say something like this: "I knew there would come a time when you would think about doing that. Making that move is an important decision, one that shouldn't be made in the heat of a fight. If that's really what you want to do, write up a plan and give it to me in a week. When I receive your written plan we will talk about it." Then walk away.

You will probably be thinking: *You mean to say that you now want to live with your father—the man who abandoned us and hasn't sent you a card or gift for your birthday or Christmas for the past three years? Not to mention the back child support he owes. You are willing to just turn your back on the person who has worked and scraped to get us by. You are the most selfish and ungrateful person I know.*

This is not the time to try to convince your child of how ungrateful he is and how much you have sacrificed for him. He won't respond to that, which would only increase your hurt, frustration, and anger.

Don't forget that the old response lurks beneath the surface! Your child's pain, his complaints, what he lacks, or your fear of blame may prompt you to revert to the old guilty response. Hang in there. Only when he realizes that you won't respond to his manipulation will he begin to change his way of coping.

Set a Date to Review the Plan

Make sure you set a date to evaluate your progress. Don't worry about feeling like you have failed. You haven't failed as long as you are still trying. Remember, what you are evaluating is the plan, not your entire worth as a human being!

Step 4: Evaluate and Modify the Plan

Evaluate the Plan

Direction

The key is whether or not you limited the amount of influence your guilt had in your life this week. If you did, then you are facing the right direction.

Expectations

Before considering how far you are from your goal, take time to look at what you did to make progress this week. Review the chart you made and see what you did well. What worked, and is there a way to do more of that?

Evaluate Your Behavior and Feelings

1. Did you feel good about your behavior?
2. With which specific goals did you succeed?
3. What did you do to make that progress?
4. Has that changed your level of anger or frustration?
5. What was hard for you?
6. What did your spouse do well?
7. Did you tell him or her?

Evaluate Your Child's Behavior and Feelings

1. Did your plan have any effect on your child?
2. Did your plan appropriately place more of your child's responsibility back on his shoulders?

Modify the Plan

After looking at what seemed to work, figure out a way to do more of that. In reviewing the chart you may find that it was very difficult to follow through on appropriate consequences. Use this information to change either the rule or the consequence.

Commit to the Revised Plan

Try the modified plan for another week and see how it works. Be sure to let at least one other person know what you are doing so he or she can encourage you and pray for you.

God gave manna to the Israelites to provide for their nourishment (Exod. 16:16–20). They were to gather the manna daily and consume it daily, except for the Sabbath. When they hung on to it so they wouldn't have to gather it the next day, it spoiled. Just as God's manna had a purpose, guilt is a helpful emotion when it pushes you to resolve situations. And just as the leftover manna spoiled, leftover guilt has many negative effects. Don't hang on to your guilt, allowing it to spoil your peace, your decisions, and your relationships. Work at keeping your guilt confessed and forgiven.

8

This Is the Last Time

Rut 3: Parental Rescuing

If, like the Prodigal Son, your younger child "collected all his belongings and went off to a foreign land where he squandered his wealth in the wildest extravagance," what would you do?

This isn't an easy question to answer. The Prodigal Son's father, however, is an excellent example of how a nonrescuing parent would respond (Luke 15:11–32). Let's compare how he handled it to what a rescuing parent would do in similar circumstances. (See table on the following page.)

Had the Prodigal's father been a Rescuer, these "helpful" actions may have allowed the Prodigal Son to limp along and maybe figure out a way to get by. However, any progress would have been contingent on Dad's continued support. As we look at this comparison, it strikes me that the rescuing parent is exerting a lot more energy—he owns the monkey—and receiving a very shaky outcome. The Prodigal Son's dad is watching, praying, and waiting. When his son returns, it is a real return—one indeed to celebrate!

Dad's Actions	Rescuing Parent's Actions
1. Allowed him to take the money and leave (vv. 12–13).	1. Beg him to stay, offering him more of the inheritance. If this doesn't work, he would offer to go along or at least send a budget or checklist.
2. Didn't pursue him to beg his return (v. 13).	2. Follow him there and help him set up his new place. Contact the neighbors to watch over him as "this is his first time away from home." Send care packages so he would have food. Pay the rent so the son wouldn't have to live with the pigs.
3. Watched for his return (v. 20).	3. Suggest he come home, provide good reasons and even Bible verses supporting his return.
4. Celebrated with him when he made a good decision to return home (vv. 22–32).	4. Worry about whether his son is going to stay home. He would reduce the expectations and demands so he won't leave again.
5. Didn't divide the inheritance again to provide money for him (v. 31).	5. Redivide the inheritance as a way of keeping him home (sibling tension guaranteed).

Let's look at how a nonrescuing mom handles her teenager.

Ironing isn't one of my wife's favorite things to do. She has found that watching T.V. while ironing makes the otherwise deplorable chore somewhat acceptable. As she irons shirts for our children, she expects them to hang them up. Individual roles are clear. Our son Mike hangs his shirts up on the floor of his room. We have pointed out flaws in his plan, but he prefers doing it that way. After a few days on the floor, however, the shirts are more wrinkled than he likes.

He then asks Bonnie to re-iron a shirt before he wears it. She offers him two choices: hang them up in the first place so they won't get wrinkled, or re-iron them yourself before you go to school. We allow him to decide–they are his shirts and he knows how he wants to look.

With these two examples in mind, let's look at the four steps to change a rescuing pattern.

Step 1: Recognize Parental Rescuing

Is This the Picture in Your Home?

Rescuing occurs when the parent removes the effect from the cause and effect, or the consequence from the behavior. Doing so on a consistent basis deprives the child of learning to modify her behavior and avoid certain painful or distasteful consequences. To teach responsibility, the parent often lectures and instructs her to act more responsibly, while continuing to remove the consequences (parent pays the fine, delivers the forgotten lunch to school, reminds of scheduled events). This results in the child acting irresponsibly, making the parent continue the pattern of rescuing (Prov. 19:19).

Rescuing frees the child from the consequences of her behavior.

If this rut operates in your family, you will probably see the following.

A child fails to learn from past mistakes. When the effect or consequence is removed, the behavior is reinforced because it has been paired with a positive outcome. If your daughter steals something and doesn't get punished, stealing becomes a way of getting something she wants without any negative effects associated with it. This may be because she didn't get caught, or because Dad's attorney got the charges dropped. Either way, the effect or consequence was removed, and she learned that stealing is a free ride.

A child fails to anticipate the consequences of her actions. The problem is that the child really doesn't have an opportunity to learn that cause and effect are linked together. She has been told (probably many times) that when she pinches her brother she will be punished. But if she is only told that and never punished, she can't be expected to change her behavior to avoid punishment. She has already avoided it!

A child expects the parents to carry the monkey in a variety of situations.

> She frequently forgets things (lunch, books, assignments). She believes it is your responsibility to produce them when needed.
> She never has any money and expects you to provide it. It really doesn't matter if your daughter runs out of money, as she believes from previous experience that you will provide more if she begs, coerces, or threatens. She probably hasn't dealt with a situation where she actually went without something because she didn't have the funds.
> Her personal items are frequently lost or misplaced. She sets them carelessly aside, assuming you will pick them up for her, or replace them if lost.
> She gives you no notice when she needs things.
> She puts things off until the last moment and then expects you to do what needs to be done to meet the deadline.

A child receives numerous school referrals, detentions, low grades, fines, or contacts from the police. Because parents don't hold her accountable for bad behavior, she assumes others won't either. She pays little attention to her actions, resulting in numerous consequences from others.

127

A child is unaware what her school assignments are and doesn't have the needed material to do them.

Parents expend increasing amounts of energy determining what the child is doing and what needs to be done about it. Parents are the ones monitoring their child's actions. Someone needs to do that and the child certainly isn't interested in the job.

Parents attend more appointments with teachers, principals, counselors, police, or probation officers to deal with the child's behavior. Parents must be involved in these meetings because they are still legally responsible for her.

Repeated Responses in Parental Rescuing

Are any of these various rescuing responses yours?

You take care of the situation. Both parent and child feel good about the parent saving the day. It's too bad that what feels good isn't helpful.

If the consequences aren't enforced, it really doesn't matter at all how severe they are.

You lecture in lieu of other natural consequences. We think if we say it just one more time, in a different way, with more sincerity, with tears, or with biblical references, she might actually get what we want her to understand.

You threaten major consequences for the next offense but do nothing for the current offense. You think that increasing the severity of the consequences will have a great influence on changing her behavior. To some degree it will, but if the consequences aren't enforced, it really doesn't matter at all how severe they are.

You protect and defend her against those who question her behavior. You call the school and get her out of trouble. You excuse her absence because she was sick, even though she wasn't. Thus you give her permission to continue her irresponsible behavior.

You blame others she was with and excuse her behavior because of their influence. Your child really didn't participate in the vandalism. "Yes, she was with the others when it occurred, but it was their negative influence that caused her to do it." If she sees that you are looking for a way to excuse her behavior, she will help you find that excuse to avoid consequences.

Let's consider the variables that may be keeping you stuck in repeated responses.

- Consider your beliefs. You may believe that

    Your child can't handle or deal with the consequences. Giving your daughter the message that she can't deal with the consequences carries with it the implicit message that she doesn't *have* to deal with the consequences. She needs to do what she can do.

    Consequences may be harmful or cause problems for your child, and thus should be avoided at all costs. Some consequences may indeed be harmful for your child. That is why it is important for her to deal with the consequences while they are small, without far-reaching implications.

    These particular consequences are too severe or unfair. If you attempt to make them more appropriate, your daughter may think you are excusing her behavior. Be clear that you only want to make them reasonable, not to excuse her actions.

- Understand your underlying motivation. Parental motivation to rescue commonly comes from the desire to:

Protect the child. There is certainly nothing wrong in wanting to protect your child. Indeed, that is an important parental function. But too much protection teaches her that decisions are free, having no cost associated with them. This is simply not true. She needs to learn how to deal with difficulties while she is still at home where you can assist her in making good decisions.

Avoid trouble. Truly there are legitimate reasons to want to keep your child out of trouble, jail, and drug treatment centers. By allowing your child the opportunity to deal with her self-created trouble when the consequences are small, she will learn to modify her behavior, keeping her out of big-time trouble in the future.

Be a good parent. You think that getting the child out of a jam is being a good parent. We all want to be good parents. But if you define being a good parent as getting her out of her own mess, you will continue to rescue her. You need to rethink this definition.

Feel good about self. You did something that your child liked and appreciated. Like the previous motivations, there is absolutely nothing wrong in wanting to feel good about yourself. However, feeling good about yourself should not be accomplished at your child's expense.

Be identified as a good parent by others in the church or at the clubhouse. I can certainly understand this one. I work with parents to help them become better parents. One of the measures of how good I am at what I do is how my own children behave. I want to look good to others and it is difficult to allow my children to make public mistakes. When they make those mistakes or poor choices they need to deal with the consequences, rather than my fixing them or sweeping them under the rug to avoid embarrassment for me.

- Examine your parents' example. Your parents may have gone to the extreme of doing too much for you. They saved you on a regular basis, causing you to believe that is what parents should do. This results in your following the same pattern with your children. Or perhaps they did too little for you. This results in your moving the other direction for your children and always being there to fix their messes.
- Study your role(s). The roles you play in your family can certainly cause you to be more protective and to rescue your children, when in reality they can handle the situation on their own.

> *Savior.* This role allows you to move in and save them from all of their hurts, pains, and struggles.
> *Proud Dad.* Your son, the star quarterback, got into a bit of a scrape with the law after Friday night's victory. You see to it that the charges are dropped so they don't interfere with his football eligibility.
> *Mother Bear.* A mother bear doesn't allow anyone to mess with her cubs. Your children need to learn how to cope with others—certainly with your support, but not with your complete control.
> *Supermom.* You assume that the problematic behavior was your fault to start with. You think, "Obviously if I had done my job properly, she wouldn't have made this bad decision in the first place." You have already assumed responsibility for the decision, so you also must assume responsibility for fixing it.

- Check your relationships. If you have sided with one of your children, it may be an expectation of that relationship that you bail her out of her problems.

Step 2: Clarify Responsibility

Parents who rescue their children typically do quite well in presenting and monitoring the family rules. They are clear in what behavior they want from their children, and do notice when the expectations are not met. However, they have trouble when it comes to enforcing the consequences. In some instances, they even interfere with the natural consequences that usually occur in a child's world.

The general rule of thumb I use is this: My child should deal with the usual and customary consequences associated with a behavior. If he gets in a fight at school, he should be suspended for three days just like every other child who fights in school. When he gets the three-day suspension, I support the school and arrange for him to do some special work during those three days rather than sleeping in and playing Nintendo all day. He probably isn't happy with that, but he learns that actions have consequences.

If I go to school and make a scene, demanding that he not be suspended, or use my influence to nullify the suspension, I have taught him that fighting is free. Do you think he will be very concerned about staying out of another fight? I think not.

On the other hand, if he gets suspended for nine days, I should be at the school asking for an explanation of the difference in punishment. If there is a reasonable explanation, and the consequence is consistent with what other students have received in similar situations, then I support the longer suspension. However, if the time was arbitrarily increased simply because someone was having a bad day, then it is my responsibility to protect my child from the longer suspension.

Determining what is rescuing and what is reasonable parental responsibility can be difficult at times. The following comparisons may help.

It's Probably Reasonable To	It's Probably Rescuing To
1. Make your child's school lunch	1. Take it to school after she forgot it for the third time this week
2. Take her to the library a week before the project is due	2. Cancel your evening's plans to take her to the library the night before the project is due
3. Remind once of chores that she needs to do	3. Do the chores for her so she doesn't get into trouble
4. Offer ideas for a report	4. Write the majority of the report
5. Remind her to collect for her paper route bill	5. Give her the money she's short to pay the newspaper office
6. Give extra chores to earn money to help pay for her car insurance	6. Pay the bill for her (so she can keep driving, even though that is not the agreement you have concerning insurance and driving)
7. Ask the whereabouts of her expensive NFL coat	7. Figure out where she left it, go find it, and bring it home, or buy her another one if it can't be found
8. Have her basketball uniform clean and available for her to wear	8. Drop her off at the game so she can warm up while you return home to pick up the uniform because she forgot it

When trying to determine if I am rescuing I usually consider two questions. Is my child physically and emotionally capable of doing the task? Am I angry about doing what I do? If he is capable of doing the task, then generally he should do it. This doesn't mean that I can't help out now and then. To most of us it feels good to be helped on occasion. But Bonnie would become resentful if she had to continually iron shirts twice. These feelings would be a cue that she is rescuing Mike from his choices. Stop doing what makes you angry and allow your child to assume his own responsibility.

Step 3: Make a Plan to Change Your Response

Determine the Goal

The rut: the child continues undesirable behaviors and you continue to rescue. The goal: to increase your child's level of responsiblity by holding her accountable for her actions. Minimally this means that you stop interfering with the natural consequences that occur from those actions.

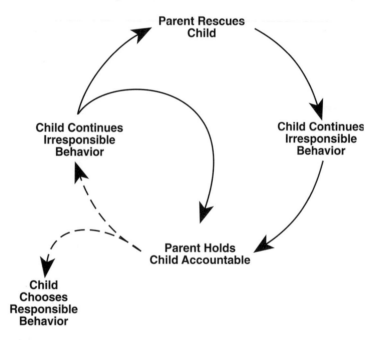

Develop a Plan

Identify Rescuing Behavior

Identify specific behaviors from which you usually save your child.

1. _____
2. _____
3. _____

Commit Yourself to Stop Rescuing

1. Review your expectations and consequences regarding those specific behaviors to make sure you and your spouse are in agreement.
2. What are the reasons that get in the way of your following through on the consequences? If you don't agree on the rule, change it so you can agree or omit it.
3. If you agree on the rule but you never follow through on the consequences, then check to see if you agree on the severity of the consequences.

Give Notice

Give notice (written or verbal) that you have stopped rescuing and that you will follow through on the stated consequences. Anticipate that you will be tested by your child to see if you meant what you said about not rescuing. Expect that she will get into trouble. Don't despair–trouble acts as a wake-up call for her to realize that she must be accountable.

Permit Child to Suffer Consequences

Permit your child to face the consequences of her actions and refuse to give in and save her. Talk with your spouse or others for support to keep from rescuing.

Abandon Protector Role

Shift from the Protector role to a Supporter role. Support your child through the consequences of her actions. One of the major jobs involved in the supportive role is to be empathetic. Empathy is communicating that you have been there and you know how it feels. That is precisely the reason Jesus can relate to us (Heb. 2:17–18).

Practice

Use the chart on the next page to practice your new responses and to limit your old ones.

Put an *X* in the corresponding days where the behavior was present. The *X*s are desirable in the top chart and undesirable in the bottom one.

Anticipate Your Child's Reaction

Your child will have an aversion to being responsible for herself. She wants you to continue to be alert and handle any situations that would adversely affect her. You will therefore likely see some of these responses.

Your child will actively hunt for new ways to pass the monkey back to you.

She will continue to expect you to save her from her problems and as a result will continue to get into trouble. She won't believe that you have changed until you don't rescue her from the consequences. When she realizes you have changed, she may be quite angry. She will say something like:

"But you've always done that. You can't change now!"
"That isn't fair. You never told me I had to take care of that."

Your response is to acknowledge how difficult it must be for her and that you will stand beside her until she successfully deals with the consequences.

She will emphatically assert that she has finally learned her lesson. She has seen the light and the error of her ways! You may hear something like:

"Mom, I really see what you've been trying to tell me. I know if I continue in this irresponsible behavior that it will ruin my chances to go to college and get a good job. But if I

Parental Behaviors

Date to evaluate: _____

Practice New Response	SUN	MON	TUES	WED	THU	FRI	SAT
Respected my child's decision by not trying to change it							
Followed through on previously agreed upon consequences, positive and negative							
Supported child to deal with the usual consequences associated with a behavior							
Supported spouse to remain firm and not give in to pressure to remove consequences							

Limit Old Response	SUN	MON	TUES	WED	THU	FRI	SAT
Nagged to complete chores or responsibilities							
Lectured about potential trouble							
Threatened major consequences, but didn't follow through							
Excused her behavior							

get an arrest record, that will affect my life for a long time. Because I really have learned my lesson, can't you just take care of this for me one last time, please? It would really mean a lot to me."

If you accept this, you run the risk of reinforcing begging and pleading as a successful way of coping.

She will attempt to make you rescue her by threatening or actually doing something to make things worse. If the situation is really bad, she may yet be able to force you into taking over. She may say: "Mom, you could fix this if you really wanted to. You won't because you don't love me. Well fine, if you don't love me, I'll just kill myself" (or variations like "run away," "get pregnant," "quit school," or "do drugs").

If you refuse to rescue her from consequences, she may increase the danger level by one of the above responses. If you then give in and remove the consequences, she has learned that a suicide or runaway threat works. Naturally she will continue to use it.

She will blame you and try to make you feel guilty for her problematic situation. You may hear:

"Why didn't you tell me about this?"
"If you would have brought my book, I wouldn't have been kicked out of class."
"If you would have excused me, I wouldn't have been marked absent."

If you buy into the guilt, you must also accept some of the responsibility for correcting the situation. Be clear in your own mind whether you should accept that guilt and obligation.

Because it is your fault that she is in this mess, she will expect you to do what needs to be done to get her out of it. Please note that she is continually trying to make you accept the monkey. She may say:

"Come on, Mom, it's only a few bucks for you, but it's my whole allowance."

"It will only take a few minutes for you to go back and pick up my stuff. You should have reminded me. If I have to go get it, I'll miss practice."

There really is no point in arguing with her about who is to blame. By arguing with you, she believes she has a chance of convincing you that it is your fault. Instead, tell her what you are willing to do and what you won't do. Then walk away and allow her to decide what she will do.

Be aware that old cues (child's irresponsible behavior, forgetting her lunch, being in jail, fear of consequences, people punishing your child) may still prompt you to return to your rescuing response. Only when your child realizes that she must deal with the situations she has created will she gradually begin to anticipate the consequences of her actions. This is a skill that she needs to develop. Your response is to encourage the skill but not to do it for her.

Set a Date to Review the Plan

Evaluating the plan with your spouse and then with your child allows you the opportunity to tell your child when she has done well and to provide appropriate consequences when she has done poorly. Having an evaluation date helps keep everyone focused on the issues. A week to ten days is generally a good trial period.

Step 4: Evaluate and Modify the Plan

Evaluate the Plan

Direction

You know you are facing the right direction if you allowed her to deal with her situation, her consequences, her struggle. Did you support her to do what she could do? One of the keys to rescuing is to determine if your child can do the behavior on her own. If she actually can do it, then she should be allowed to do it herself.

Expectations

Take time to review what went well, so you can do more of that. Review the chart you made, to feel good about your progress.

Evaluate Your Behavior and Feelings

1. Did you feel good about your behavior?
2. With which specific goals did you succeed?
3. What did you do to make that progress?
4. Has that changed your level of anger or frustration?
5. What was hard for you?
6. What did your spouse do well?
7. Did you tell him or her?

Evaluate Your Child's Behavior and Feelings

1. Did your plan have any effect on your child?
2. Did your plan appropriately place more of your child's responsibility back on her shoulders?

Modify the Plan

Determine the specific cues that still prompt you to fall into your rescuing behavior. Be aware of these for the coming week. Plan an alternative response for those cues.

Commit to the Revised Plan

Set a date and time about a week away to review the new plan.

We think we are being benevolent by giving our child one more chance. Actually we are doing harm by reinforcing irresponsible behavior. Having to deal with the consequence helps her to decide if she made a good decision. Without that evaluation, she will very likely repeat the behavior.

When the pattern has been established that the parent(s) will rescue the child from consequences, it is difficult to break because the child isn't learning from past mistakes. Saving the day makes us parents feel good about ourselves, and it is difficult for us to find an acceptable point at which to stop rescuing. There is a tendency for the child's behavior to get worse and naturally the consequences become more severe. Because of the increased severity, we tell ourselves that we will bail her out just once more. Furthermore, the child often means it at the time when she says, "I have learned my lesson and it will never happen again. Please, just this one last time?"

If you are a Rescuer, at some point you will be unable to prevent severe consequences from occurring, which will truly be unfair to your child. She didn't have an opportunity to practice handling the consequences when they were minor, when mistakes would not have been so costly. The crucial principle is this: Now is the time to stop rescuing!

9

I Just Can't Do It

Rut 4: Parental Weakness or Absence

Eli, the Old Testament priest, knew his sons were messing up. He knew how his boys were living, but instead of doing what he needed to do, Eli chose to deal with the problem by lecturing them. He did what he always did (lecture), and of course he got what he usually got—his sons ignored him.

> Why do you do such things, the evil things that I hear from all these people? No, my sons; for the report is not good which I hear the LORD's people circulating. If one man sins against another, God will mediate for him; but if a man sins against the LORD, who can intercede for him?
>
> 1 Samuel 2:23–25

Like most parents who have little follow-through, Eli's lectures were attempts to control his children's behavior through guilt and fear. Even lecturing about spiritual matters was not effective. The Scripture gives a clear message: When words are not sufficient to correct a situation, parents have a responsibility to take appropriate action.

I have told [Eli] that I am about to judge his house forever for the iniquity which he knew, because his sons brought a curse on themselves and he did not rebuke them.

1 Samuel 3:13

God gave Eli the responsibility to do more than talk, but Eli's weakness prevented change from occurring. He failed to provide needed direction.

Similarly, parents who are absent cannot provide that direction for their children. Some single dads survive the pain of divorce and subsequent separation by not maintaining contact with their children. They drop the contact, not because they don't love their children, but because they can't cope with the emotional strain of having to say good-bye at the end of each visit. When this occurs, the children miss out on needed fatherly influence. Of course, the dad also misses out on the joy of seeing his children mature.

Turning to another scriptural example, we see that the disciples were positively influenced because they had been with Jesus.

Now as they observed the confidence of Peter and John, and understood that they were uneducated and untrained men, they were marveling, and began to recognize them as having been with Jesus.

Acts 4:13

Obviously, the opportunity to influence your children is much greater when you are with them, both emotionally and physically.

Step 1: Recognize Parental Weakness or Absence

Is This the Picture in Your Home?

The striking feature of this rut is the lack of positive parental direction in the child's life caused by parental weakness or absence. Every child needs that direction and when he doesn't receive it, he fills the void by making his own decisions.

When parental direction isn't provided, children determine their own way.

Parental weakness is characterized by the parent's unwillingness to make a clear, firm stand and to back it up with more than just words—Eli's problem. The weak parent gives in to the child's demands. Roles are often reversed: The child acts in the parent role, with the parent trying to meet the child's expectations.

Parental absence occurs in a variety of situations. Some parents have jobs that take them away from their children for a day, a week, or even months, while others have abandoned their children and haven't communicated for years. Yet some parents may be physically present every day, but emotionally unavailable. Their energy to parent is being stolen by other areas of their lives such as job, recreation, social life, church involvement. Obviously it is more difficult to provide direction for your child if you aren't present, either physically or emotionally, to do the job.

Because parental input and direction are not given, the child is left to his own devices to cope with life. If this rut operates in your family, you will probably see the following.

A child has poor problem-solving skills. Left to himself, he resorts to trial and error problem solving. He needs to understand how his parents work through a problem.

A child makes numerous mistakes without parental guidance. He simply doesn't have the experience or wisdom to make good decisions by himself. He makes decisions based on what feels good for the moment. Parents need to provide guidelines for him until he is able to make good decisions for himself (Deut. 6:7–9; Eph. 6:4).

A child seeks direction from other children. Because parents don't provide the needed direction, the child frequently looks to peers for his bearings. He may become quite dependent upon them and may follow them into unhealthy activities.

A child has problems with those in authority. Because the child has become quite used to making his own decisions, he expects those outside of the home will also defer to his decisions. He thinks others simply don't have the right or authority to tell him what to do. Directions from those in authority are disregarded, resulting in further trouble.

A parent receives pressure from outsiders—teachers, counselors, principals, police—to control the child. People call to inform parents of problems with the implicit message that the parents should control their child.

Repeated Responses in Parental Weakness or Absence

Instead of providing the needed direction, it is easy for parents to get stuck in these unproductive rut responses.

Avoid situations requiring decisions. Because weak parents believe they can't make good decisions or follow through on them, they avoid situations that require parental decisions.

Get other people to make the decisions. The weak parent isn't sure what to do, so it is easy to defer to the experts who seem to know what is best for the child. The parent will agree with almost anything that is recommended, but seldom follows through with his or her part of the plan. When a parent is absent, he or she may indirectly force others to make decisions through the vacuum created by the absence.

Defer to the child's judgment. Always allowing the child to make the decision minimizes parent-child conflict. The strongest directive usually given to a child by a weak parent is, "Do what you want." If the parent permits him to do whatever he wants to do, he may be happy, but he won't be learning the necessary skills to survive in the world. In the case of the absent parent, the child simply does what he wants to do.

Find a strong mate who will take a firm hand with the children. This frequently occurs in stepfamilies. The single parent may look for a mate who will bring discipline and order to the family. Stepfamilies are often formed when the teenagers are beginning to rebel. The biological parent thinks that another parent figure would calm the rebellion and add some stability to the family. Unfortunately, the rebellious teenager is not about to accept limits without a fight from this new stranger who lives at his house!

Leave when things get too difficult. Leaving eliminates the immediate stress, and allows the parent to do what he or she wants–without parental responsibilities.

Make completely unrealistic directives. Because the input is so far from being acceptable, the absent parent's demands are quickly and easily dismissed by the entire family.

Did any of this sound familiar? Think about the following factors that may keep you locked into one of these repeated responses.

- Consider your beliefs. Beliefs that are frequently present in the weak parent's mind include

    I don't know what to do
    If I did something, it would be wrong
    I don't want to cause any harm by making a wrong
        decision
    I'm not as strong as my child
    My child wouldn't listen to or respect my decisions
        anyway

  The absent parent believes

    I shouldn't make a decision because I'm not there
        to help carry it out
    Because I'm gone, my child wouldn't listen to what
        I say anyway

My ex-spouse won't enforce my rules while I'm gone

These beliefs may or may not be true but they certainly should be discussed and resolved.

- Understand your underlying motivation. The weak parent may want to

  Avoid involvement
  Avoid conflict and turmoil
  Avoid being exposed as weak or wrong
  Avoid painful emotions associated with relationship
  Have peace at almost any cost

  The absent parent may want to

  Avoid involvement
  Be actively involved with the family but doesn't know how to do so
  Avoid the repeated sense of loss associated with frequent hellos and good-byes

- Examine your parents' example. How did your parents give you the direction you needed? Perhaps they made every decision for you. If this occurred, you are quite likely to want to give your child more breathing room. But be alert to when he needs a little more direction. Or perhaps they told you nothing and left you to your own resources. If this occurred, you may be inclined to provide too much direction. Be sensitive to his need for more or less parental direction.
- Study your role(s). Does your role dictate behavior that is inconsistent with providing direction for your children?

  Disneyland Dad. He picks up the kids and takes them out for a wonderful time. He is most concerned about whether they still like him. Giving them direction may upset them, so he won't risk that.

Ghost. When any direction or decision is needed, this parent disappears. It may be a physical disappearance—leaves for a few days, or an emotional disappearance—checks out and won't talk about the issue.

Pal. This parent wants to be the child's best friend. I often hear this statement, "We can talk about anything; we are best friends." There is nothing wrong with being friendly with your child, but setting some firm parental limits can only be done by an effectively functioning parent.

- Check your relationships. If you are sided with one of your children, it may be extremely difficult to assert yourself and disagree with what he wants. Remember, your child needs clear direction from you, with appropriate consequences enforced.

Step 2: Clarify Responsibility

Parental weakness or absence greatly interferes with your parental responsibility to present, monitor, and enforce your family rules.

Present Expectations

The weak parent doesn't present rules. That would start something she doesn't believe she could maintain. At most, she offers suggestions as alternatives to the child's current behavior. These suggestions are rarely listened to, much less followed.

The absent parent may leave firm rules that he expects his wife and children to follow. Usually the mom thinks these rules are too strict so she doesn't enforce them. Thus it doesn't matter what is presented.

Monitor Compliance

The weak parent doesn't really want to know what is happening because she would then need to respond in some fashion. This is not something she is ready to do. Ignorance is bliss.

Not being at home, the absent parent is physically incapable of monitoring what occurs there.

Enforce Consequences

The weak parent believes she is incapable of enforcing anything, and doesn't.

The absent parent cannot enforce anything because he isn't there to make sure it gets done. He can tell his teenager not to use the phone, but in his absence, the teen's social urging, or rebellion, will overcome the parental limit.

Having to take action is frightening to parents who feel more comfortable with simply talking. Acting clarifies responsibility, placing the monkey appropriately on the child's back. Let's look at a hypothetical situation and examine the difference between talking and acting.

Your son refuses to do his chores. After discussing it, you and your spouse agree that he won't play with his friends unless his chores are done. You have both talked to him about the rule and have given him a few breaks but he continues to avoid his chores. Today is a beautiful sunny day. Your son arrives home after a tough day at school and decides to watch a little television. He is about to do his chores—so he says—when his friends arrive asking if he can go out to play. "I'll do my chores as soon as I get done playing. I'll just be gone forty-five minutes. May I go, Mom, please?"

Decision time is upon you. You think back and remember the broken promises and your agreement with your spouse, and decide to stand firm and put the monkey on the child's back. Because he is now motivated to get something he wants, he argues with you and asks why he must do his

Getting Out of Those Ruts

chores now. He gives you several reasons why the chores aren't fair anyway. You are now at a point where you can continue to talk or you can act. He knows that if he can keep the argument going he has a chance to get what he wants. What should you do?

Tell his friends that he is unable to play now and that they will have to come back later.

Do you see how that would change the situation? Your son would know that you are serious about his chores, and that he is now the owner of the monkey. A checklist may be helpful for you when you are moving from words to action.

> Did you give him the message you wanted him to have?
> Did you give the message in the least embarrassing way for him?
> Did you withhold any barbs or jabs that might have invited him to fight with you?
> Were the points of choice and responsibility clear?

Go back and examine your action. You sent the friends away, a clear message that you meant what you said about the chores. He got the message you wanted him to get. You made no negative comments about his character or work habits. Looks like you took appropriate action! So far so good. What you aren't sure of is how he is going to respond.

Your son clearly has a choice to make. He can decide to do his chores or not to do them. If he does his chores, you'll permit him to join his friends. If he doesn't do them, he is experiencing the agreed-upon consequences. However, this may not be the end of this interaction. What will you do if your son punches a hole in the door of his room? This is an attempt to pass the monkey back to you. It will work if you allow him to convince you that punching the hole was your fault—how can you hold him responsible for his actions when you sent his friends away?

150

What happens if he tries to leave anyway—another monkey attempt? Inform him that he is now at another choice point—monkey to son. If he tries to leave, you will stop him, call the police, or whatever you have previously made clear to him. The important thing is that whatever decision he makes, he must know that you will hold him responsible for his choices. If he punches a hole in the door, he must pay for the repair or replace the door.

Step 3: Make a Plan to Change Your Response

Determine the Goal

The goal is for the parent to positively reinvolve himself with his children. Because paternal absence is a frequent topic in counseling sessions, I strongly encourage fathers to return to their children. There are two major reasons why they should return and reconnect.

First, a father is the only one who can give his input. A father's input and evaluation are crucially important to the child. Others can say good things about him, but what does his father say? Everyone else in the world (except for Mom) can find a substitute for himself or herself. There is no one who can substitute for a father or a mother. This is not to say that a stepparent can't move into a father or mother role. Indeed they can, but that doesn't negate the child's need to know what the biological parent thinks of him.

Second, if you don't give your input, your child will reach some conclusion as to why you didn't stick around to do so. There are three major conclusions from which children usually choose: There is something drastically wrong with me (damaged goods); I did something terribly wrong; or, Dad is a jerk. A child frequently starts with feeling there is something drastically wrong with him, but as counseling progresses he concludes that Dad is a jerk. This certainly may be an incorrect conclusion but without input from his dad, it is hard to reach any other one.

Your family should be pleased that you have returned to be a positive influence in their lives–but they may not feel that way immediately. You see, they have established a routine without you. To include you they will have to make a space for you to fill, and some duties for you to perform. The space and duties need to be negotiated with some sensitivity. In many counseling situations I have seen a returning dad reverse every decision Mom made in his absence and lay down the law to his teenagers by giving them a stern lecture and extending their grounding period.

Whoa! How do you think that worked? Did Dad reinvolve himself with the family? Well, yes he did, but certainly not in a positive way. They were angry and resentful at what he did, causing the whole family to unite against him. This further alienated him from the family–the opposite of what he wanted to accomplish.

So the goal then is to modify the parent's response to a positive reinvolvement with his family, as shown in the diagram on the following page.

Develop a Plan

Assess the Situation

Talk with other family members to find out what is occurring. How do they feel about the situation? What is each member doing? How is it working?

What are your strengths?

How would the situation improve if you used your strengths?

An apology may be appropriate for your lack of previous involvement.

Address Your Hindrances

What is interfering with your making a positive contribution to the situation? For example:

If you don't know how to set restrictions on unacceptable behavior, attend a parenting class

If you are coping with a divorce by avoiding contact with your family, attend a divorce seminar to help you reestablish contact with your children

If your schedule doesn't allow time with your children, modify your schedule where possible

Talk with the other parent about how you can have an influence even though you are away—telephone calls, postcards, letters addressing specific issues that are pertinent to what is happening at home

Establish a Structure for Involvement

Because you are increasing your active involvement with them—changing direction—it would be helpful to advise them so they can adapt to the change.

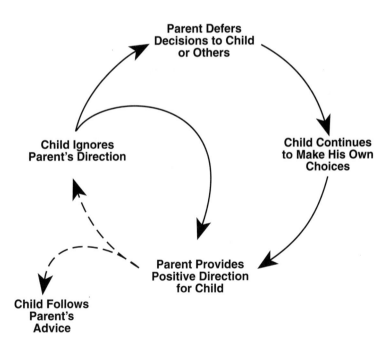

Develop a structure that you can follow—"We will talk about family issues at supper on Tuesday." An important part of this structure is your consistent contact. If you are a divorced father, it is more important to consistently see your child on a weekly basis, rather than daily for two weeks and then not at all for two months, whenever distance allows. Your child needs to know what he can count on.

To ease the transition back into the home or into your child's life, establish a way to find out what happened while you were gone, assess what needs your attention, and give your input without undermining what your spouse has done.

Follow through on your promise! Because of your lack of previous involvement, you will also need to be persistent until your child recognizes that you are there for the long run. Don't give up.

Practice

Use the chart on the following page to practice your new responses and limit your old ones.

Put an X in the corresponding days where the behavior was present. The Xs are desirable in the top chart and undesirable in the bottom one.

Anticipate Your Child's Reaction

It is doubtful that your child—or the other parent—will be pleased when you provide needed direction. Your child won't like the changes that you make.

Your child will actively resist your input.

He may ignore your input. He probably heard it, but just decided to ignore it. He may covertly be saying, "So what are you going to do about it?" Think carefully before going for a power play, as they generally don't work well in these situations. But be persistent.

Parental Behaviors

Date to Evaluate: _____

Practice New Response	SUN	MON	TUES	WED	THU	FRI	SAT
Involved myself in decisions concerning the children							
Made time in my schedule to include them							
Attempted to gain needed information and skills to work with them							
Identified and used my strengths to involve myself with my children							

Limit Old Response	SUN	MON	TUES	WED	THU	FRI	SAT
Kept thoughts and ideas to myself							
Deferred decisions to others or to my children							
Emotionally or physically checked out							
Didn't make consistent contact while I was gone							

He may angrily point out your lack of previous involvement. From his perspective, he needed your influence earlier in his life when he had no idea what to do. Now that he is older and has figured some things out, he doesn't need or want your help. Your willingness to be involved now doesn't offset his anger at your lack of a timely response when he really needed it. You will probably hear comments similar to these: "I don't need your advice now! I don't want your guidance! I'll tell you when I needed it. I needed it three years ago when I didn't know what to do . . . So keep your ideas to yourself and leave me alone!"

He may be angry at you for showing interest now. Parents often decide to take a stand on an issue that the child wants to handle himself (dating, sex, drinking). He knows the direction he wants to take and doesn't want input from his parents. You will hear comments like: "You didn't want to help me with the problem I was having, even though I asked and asked. But now you are sticking your nose into my business and it doesn't belong there. If I wanted your opinion on who to date, I would have asked. It's none of your business! It's my life, so go back to where you came from."

He may assert that he can take care of himself now. He believes that he can take care of himself and doesn't need your help. You will hear comments like: "Just in case you haven't noticed, I've been making my own decisions for the past four years. And I think I'm doing a pretty good job. I don't want or need your help now."

Remember that the old rut responses are prowling about, waiting for an opportunity to reemerge. A difficult parental decision, a long business trip, or your child's refusal to listen to your direction may make it easy for you to check out of the situation again. Only when he sees that you must be reckoned with will he begin to accept your input. You must be consistent with your involvement and be willing to listen more than you talk.

Set a Date to Review the Plan

Make sure that you follow through on the evaluation of the plan on the date scheduled. It is easy to let it go, especially if things seem to be going pretty well. Parents like Eli often ask why questions when things go poorly. I also try to ask questions when things go well because it gives me a chance to reinforce what is working.

"What motivated you to make those good grades?"

"What did you do so that you were able to make it in by your curfew?"

"Why did you get along so well with your sister this morning?"

Step 4: Evaluate and Modify the Plan

Evaluate the Plan

Direction

You are facing the right direction if you involved yourself more with your child. It may mean that you simply asked a few more questions, or didn't accept the "Fine" answer to your question about his day. Look for ways to increase your contact with your child. Remember, it is much more difficult to have an impact if you aren't with him.

Expectations

Take time to review what went well, so you can do more of that. Review the chart you made, to feel good about your progress.

Evaluate Your Behavior and Feelings

1. Did you feel good about your behavior?
2. With which specific goals did you succeed?

157

3. What did you do to make that progress?
4. Has that changed your level of anger or frustration?
5. What was hard for you?
6. What did your spouse do well?
7. Did you tell him or her?

Evaluate Your Child's Behavior and Feelings

1. Did your plan have any effect on your child?
2. Did your plan appropriately place more of your child's responsibility back on his shoulders?

Modify the Plan

What part of the plan seemed to work the best? Keep that part! Where did you struggle? Can you change that part somehow?

Commit to the Revised Plan

Once again, try the plan for a week to ten days and see what occurs. Don't get discouraged if you need to modify the plan several times. Each change gives you more information and moves you closer to a workable solution.

The only person in the world who can provide your input is you. You have unique strengths to contribute to the growth and development of your children. Use those strengths for their well-being and for yours!

10

I'm Stuck in the Middle

Rut 5: Parental Mediating

Sally and Sam have problems with Sally's fourteen-year-old son Charlie completing his regular chores. Charlie gets fifteen dollars per week for emptying the trash and cleaning up after the dog in the backyard. If Charlie kept up with his chores, they would only take a few minutes each day to complete.

Sam says to Charlie, "You know, I was thinking about your chores. You might try doing them right after you get home from school, before you get your snack. That way you could get them done and out of the way before you relaxed. They wouldn't interfere with your homework, you wouldn't have to think about them again the whole evening, nor would you forget them. That's the way I try to do certain things at work. I get the things done that I don't like early in the morning, and then they don't interfere with the rest of my day. What do you think about that idea?"

Charlie replies, "I dunno, yeah maybe."

Sally says to Sam, "I think it would be best if you just left him alone. Didn't we already talk about his chores this morning? I thought you agreed not to mention them, and besides

Charlie is doing better–he did his chores twice this week." (Unfortunately this is already Friday.)

Charlie smiles and begins to think about the movie he wants to see tonight.

Sam responds to Sally, "Okay, okay, I was just trying to be helpful. If Charlie did his chores and earned his allowance, he wouldn't have to worry about financing his weekend activities. You don't seem to care whether he learns any responsibility or not." Sam angrily walks away.

Charlie's smile evaporates as he thinks about having to pay for the movie himself. Only one thing to do now: "Mom, can you advance me a little from my allowance so I can go to the movie? All of my friends are going. I'll do all my chores next week, I promise!"

"Okay, but I am not kidding, you will do all of your chores next week, right?"

"Right, Mom!"

"And why can't you be more respectful toward Sam? He is just trying to help. If only the two of you would get along, this would be a much better place to live. He helps pay your allowance so you should treat him better."

Sam returns and says to Charlie, "Maybe we could think about a couple ways for you to save money so you wouldn't have to keep borrowing from your mother. I have found that it works best to put a little away first, before spending any of my paycheck. I would be glad to help you plan a budget. You really should be saving some of your money."

Charlie replies, "I dunno, yeah maybe."

Sally to Sam: "Will you just leave him alone! Why are you always on his case?"

Sam regularly offers hints to Charlie to help him become more responsible. Charlie resents his stepdad and his helpful hints, and conveniently forgets to do his chores. Sally thinks that Sam is too critical of Charlie so she makes excuses for her son, even when she knows Sam is right. She pushes Charlie to be more respectful toward Sam, but makes little progress.

Sally and Sam share a common goal: They want Charlie to become a responsible young man. Their current pattern of Sam's hinting and Sally's excusing isn't working. A viable recycled response might be for Sally to assume responsibility for monitoring Charlie's chores. Instead of trying to keep Sam and Charlie from hassling each other, she could clearly state what she expects from Charlie. Part of the reason he doesn't want to do his chores is because he likes irritating Sam. With his mother monitoring his chores, being negligent won't be as gratifying. Furthermore, with Mom in charge of the chores, she will likely stop excusing his poor effort, and won't advance money for chores he hasn't completed. These changes would help Charlie assume more responsibility.

Step 1: Recognize Parental Mediation

Is This the Picture in Your Home?

In this rut, Sally and other Mediators have two major jobs: regulating the tension between the parent and child, and keeping the family together. The third party's willingness to mediate may prevent a feared breakup of the family, but can limit the investment the other two have in working toward resolution. The need for a Mediator is quite strong in the following family situations.

There is extreme similarity between a parent and child. Because the parent and child are so similar in personality and coping style, they are constantly at odds with each other. I frequently hear the statement, "We are exactly alike–that's why we can't get along with each other." Typical examples of this are a parent and child who both want to have the last word, are perfectionistic–but not in the same way–or want to control things and be in charge. The resulting tension causes the other parent to step in and mediate.

There is conflict between a parent and child. The tension is escalating, requiring the other parent to mediate.

The family is a stepfamily. The biological parent mediates between the stepparent and the children. If both partners in the marriage have biological children living in the family, they may both be mediating on behalf of their children.

If this rut occurs in your family—whether you're a single parent, two parents, or a stepparent—you will probably see the following.

The Mediator owning the monkey. Sally sacrifices her own desires, needs, and sometimes her principles to keep both sides happy. Often there is no flexibility to negotiate from either of the sides. As a result, any giving needs to be done by the Mediator. The Mediator works the hardest, expending the most energy.

Frequent power struggles between the two warring parties. Each wants to win or prove the other wrong. Seldom does either side walk away from an argument—no matter how trivial.

Lack of parental unity. Sally doesn't believe she could firmly unite with Sam without harming or losing Charlie. Typically, the parents aren't in agreement about what is occurring, making it difficult for them to work together.

A constant underlying pressure for the family to split. The tension reaches such a level that anything that would reduce it becomes a viable option.

An exhausted Mediator. This is a very difficult task, requiring much energy and willingness to compromise. Unfortunately, most of Sally's energy is used in areas where she has no control. If the warring parties aren't willing to work on their relationship, there is little she can do to make them get along. But she keeps trying! The call to the counselor is made when the Mediator is exhausted and the family is on the verge of breaking apart.

Repeated Responses in Parental Mediating

In an attempt to keep the peace and hold the family together, it is easy for the Mediator and the two parties to get stuck in repeated rut responses.

The Mediator covers for both sides to reduce sources of tension. Sally may cover for Charlie by secretly doing his chores to prevent Sam from being angry about Charlie's lack of responsibility. Sally may cover for Sam by not imposing the full two-week grounding period, trying to make him look less negative.

The Mediator constantly negotiates to improve the position of each party. Sally points out to Sam the chores Charlie has done without being reminded. She points out to Charlie the positive things that happen to him because Sam really does care about him.

The Mediator works to keep things balanced. Sam and Charlie pull at Sally to make sure each gets his fair share of her time and attention. If they aren't attended to on a relatively equal basis, one of them might decide to leave. To avoid that, Sally is highly attentive to them both.

One or both of the warring parties threatens to leave. Sam's and Charlie's commitment to work through the problems with each other is minimal. Because each side may be committed only to the Mediator, they purposely do things to irritate the other side. Charlie may ruin the marital relationship for Mom by driving Sam away. Similarly, Sam may figure out a way to send Charlie to his biological father. The threat to leave is a way of getting the Mediator to clamp down more firmly on the other party. Naturally if the threat works, it will continue to be used.

You know it's getting tense when you hear statements like these:

"I guess we both can't live here."
"The only solution is for one of us to leave."

163

"You (Mediator) have to choose who you want to live in this house."

The two parties take cheap shots at each other. Because they don't think they have any power to change things, they resort to venting their frustration on each other. Each may also believe that creating enough turmoil may be a way of getting rid of the other one.

Did any of this sound familiar? Think about the factors that may keep you locked into one of these responses.

- Consider your beliefs. The Mediator usually believes some of the following:

  The two parties should fervently love each other—not just coexist
  If left alone, the warring parties would have a huge blowup, causing irreparable damage
  It's up to me to prevent a family split

  The warring parties often believe

  There is nothing I can do to change the other party
  The Mediator won't make the other party behave
  Things aren't going to change, so I have to live with this or leave

  Regardless of whether these beliefs are true or false, they will have a powerful influence on behavior. Determining the verity of the beliefs may allow parents a way to move beyond impasse.

- Understand your underlying motivation. The Mediator usually wants to

  Have harmonious relationships in the family
  Assuage guilt by having smooth interactions among family members

Make things better for both parties so they will be more cooperative and will want to improve their relationship

Those in the warring parties may each want to

Make a positive contribution to the other's life
Have his or her own point of view understood and appreciated
Get the Mediator to take his or her side
Express anger toward the Mediator
Show the other party he or she is wrong
Get rid of the other party

Talking about the underlying motivation with your spouse may promote parental unity.

- Examine your parents' example. Two extreme parental pictures may influence your response. In your growing-up family, you may have had a parent who always mediated between you and your other parent. Unfortunately, this may make it easy for you to do the same, preventing the warring parties from working through their difficulties themselves. Or you may have had a parent who never mediated between you and your other parent. Because you may be following the example to never step in, be aware of times when your spouse is temporarily off balance and needs help dealing with the child.
- Study your role(s).

  Peacemaker. If you were a Peacemaker in your family of origin, it will be very easy for you to assume a parental mediator position in your current family.
  Disciplinarian. Does your role prevent you from establishing a bond with the child? Does it keep you from walking away from a potential fight?

- Check your relationships. If you are the family Mediator, it is quite likely that you and your spouse disagree about rules and consequences for your child. Working through these disagreements with your spouse is essential, particularly if you are unusually close to this child.

Step 2: Clarify Responsibility

Present Expectations

Clear rules are not presented because the parents disagree on rules or consequences.

Monitor Compliance

The Mediator monitors the relationship, not the rules, so things won't get out of hand. The warring parent, in turn, monitors the Mediator's lack of rule enforcement. He or she focuses on the negative in the child and often misses the positives.

Enforce Consequences

The Mediator frequently softens the consequences imposed by the other parent. Consequently there's nothing to enforce, except the peace.

Step 3: Make a Plan to Change Your Response

Determine the Goal

The goal is for the two people to work out their differences without depending on the third party to mediate for them. To change the rut, the Mediator must change his or her response as shown on the following page.

Develop a Plan

Mediator Must Determine a Stand

In her attempt to keep the family together, Sally's thoughts and wishes are often lost.

What rules and expectations do you have?
How would you like to handle certain problem situations?
What makes it difficult for you to speak up?

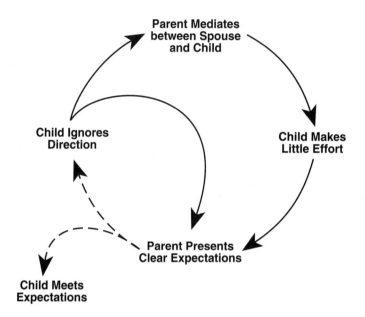

The Mediator must speak up and voice an opinion rather than waiting for the warring parent to initiate the conversation. This can be a difficult step for the Mediator.

The Mediator should be the one to suggest an appropriate consequence or reward.

For example, because of his role, Sam frequently decides Charlie's punishment. Sally then tries to soften the consequence so it will be more acceptable to Charlie. Instead, the Mediator should be the one to suggest an appropriate consequence or reward and to discuss it with the other parent.

Parents Must Reach Agreement

The need for a mediator indicates that parents are not in agreement. In the long run if parents aren't together, the family probably won't survive. The Mediator needs to reach agreement with the other parent so they can present a united front to the child.

Unfortunately, the Mediator often tries to make the needed adjustments with the child, rather than with the other parent.

For example, Dad mediates between Mom and daughter who are "just alike." The daughter misbehaves and Mom grounds her for a month. Dad and of course the daughter think this is too long. Instead of going to his spouse and working out their disagreement, Dad dismisses the last two weeks of his daughter's grounding.

Mom imposed a consequence, but Dad prevented overkill. Balance was achieved because the daughter knew she did something wrong but also knew she was loved and forgiven. This process, though, left Mom and Dad upset with each other. Dad should have gone to his wife first to find this balance.

Mediator Must Stop Mediating

This may include some or all of the following:

Advise the parties that he or she will no longer buffer their relationship
Stop relaying messages between the two parties
Focus on individual needs rather than on keeping the peace
Teach negotiation skills
Set clear guidelines on what she will do, and not do
Set limits, complete with consequences, on certain behaviors

Warring Parent Must Look for Positives

The warring parent must find positives in the child and verbalize them to the child and to the Mediator. If Sam stopped trying to change Charlie and focused on finding positives in him, Sally would be pleased. This would reduce the tension between Sam and Charlie and would allow Sally to take a firmer stand with her son. Charlie wouldn't get as big a kick out of avoiding his chores if his mom were upset with him rather than his stepdad.

Warring Parent Must Avoid Lesser Issues

Sam must determine critical issues that are worth fighting about and walk away from the other power struggles. If Charlie wants to pick a fight with him, any issue will do–from the crucial to the trivial and stupid. Charlie thus picks at least some fights over nonessential issues. If Sam would walk away from those fights, the conflict would be considerably reduced.

Find positives in the child and verbalize them.

Unfortunately, the warring parent often feels like he or she must respond to the challenge and fight about everything– a victory is a victory even if it is over something ridiculous. Determine which issues are not crucial and walk away. It's okay to leave the kid standing there arguing by himself! Here are several examples that Sally and Sam determined were nonessential and essential issues for Charlie.

Nonessential Issues	Essential Issues
Wearing matching clothes to school	Wearing clothes to school
Wearing a shirt and tie to church	Wearing a shirt and going to church
Dusting his room every Saturday	Being able to walk into his room
Doing chores enthusiastically	Doing chores
Getting up in time to eat breakfast before going to school	Catching the bus

169

The important part of any issue is that parents agree on the essential versus the nonessential.

Practice

Use the chart on the following page to practice your new responses and limit your old ones.

Put an *X* in the corresponding days where the behavior was present. The *X*s are desirable in the top chart and undesirable in the bottom one.

Anticipate Your Child's Reaction

If you begin to limit your mediating, your child will likely respond in some of the following ways.

Increasing the amount of trouble he causes. By doing this he is providing more reasons for the warring parent to be angry at him. When the spouse is upset, the mediator must work even harder to keep things calmed down. Behaviorally the child is pushing you to continue mediating. If you respond to this, you could be stuck mediating indefinitely.

Increasing the number of complaints about the other parent. He wants you to know all that is wrong, so you will continue to watch out for him and protect him. This obviously keeps you squarely in the middle of the conflict. It is important to discuss and resolve these issues directly and privately with the other parent, so you don't continue to balance things out with the child (like the dad who reduced his daughter's grounding).

Threatening to leave—either by running away or wanting to live with someone else. He wants to make sure that you keep the other parent in line so he (the child) doesn't feel mistreated enough to leave.

Pulling other people into the middle. To ensure he has someone to mediate for him, he may pull in other adults (grandparents, aunts, uncles, teachers, counselors, family service workers).

Remember that old prompts are still present to keep you mediating. Limiting those responses will help him realize

Parental Behaviors

Date to evaluate: _____

Practice New Response	SUN	MON	TUES	WED	THU	FRI	SAT
Consulted and negotiated with spouse instead of balancing things out with child							
Clearly stated my opinion							
Set appropriate limits on what I would do							
Focused on individual needs (theirs and mine)							
Encouraged them to work out problems directly with each other, and left							

Limit Old Response	SUN	MON	TUES	WED	THU	FRI	SAT
Mediated their difficulties							
Did all of the adjusting or accommodating							
Worked harder than anyone else to make things peaceful							
Didn't do anything for myself							

that you mean business. Once he sees this, he will begin to try new ways of coping.

Set a Date to Review the Plan

Set a specific time and date to review the plan (approximately seven to ten days from when you implement it). Whether the plan worked poorly or very well, take time to evaluate it!

Step 4: Evaluate and Modify the Plan

Evaluate the Plan

Direction

Did you make suggestions for possible consequences and rewards for your child's behavior? Did you offer your input rather than try to soften your spouse's response? You know you are facing the right direction if you spoke up and expected both parties to take your opinion seriously.

Expectations

Before considering how far you are from your goal, take time to look at what you did to make progress this week. Review the chart you made and see what you did well. What worked, and is there a way to do more of that?

Evaluate Your Behavior and Feelings

1. Did you feel good about your behavior?
2. With which specific goals did you succeed?
3. What did you do to make that progress?
4. Has that changed your level of anger or frustration?
5. What was hard for you?
6. What did your spouse do well?
7. Did you tell him or her?

Evaluate Your Child's Behavior and Feelings

1. Did your plan have any effect on your child?
2. Did your plan appropriately place more of your child's responsibility back on her shoulders?

Modify the Plan

Given your responses to the preceding evaluation questions, how can you modify your plan so it will be more productive? Make changes that will allow you to feel good about your responsibilities and will place the monkey appropriately on your child's back.

Commit to the Revised Plan

Make the needed modifications and commit to the new plan for a specified period. Set a date to evaluate your revisions.

Frequently in stepfamilies there are unresolved loss or grief issues that need to be addressed. Charlie can't fully accept Sam until Charlie has worked through his feelings concerning the absence of his biological father. Until that is accomplished, he is in no mood to get along with Sam.

People must work through their own disagreements. Continuing to mediate won't solve the problem. Mediating with more fervor won't remove the conflict from the relationship. The Mediator must shift out of the usual response and be more assertive concerning his or her expectations.

11

My Child Is Different

Rut 6: The Special Needs Child

Pam (mother of twelve-year-old boy) says, "I don't know what else to do! Nothing works. We've tried everything. We've taken everything away from him and it doesn't seem to matter. Even though he's a smart boy, he's getting terrible grades. He's a behavior problem at school, and his teacher says he has an 'attention span of about five minutes.' He doesn't do his chores unless I nag him. Consequences don't matter to him. What am I supposed to do? Tell me and I will do it."

Step 1: Recognize the Special Needs Child

Is This the Picture in Your Home?

The child with special needs—attention deficit disorder (ADD), asthma, severe depression, fetal alcohol syndrome, diabetes, or other disability—is not easy to parent. Over-focusing or underfocusing on the problem usually causes an escalation of symptoms, and achieving proper balance is challenging. Much turmoil exists for the child, the parents, and the rest of the family. The difficulty can demand more and more attention, thus limiting available energy for positive growth. If you have one of these children in your family, you probably see or experience the following.

Overfocusing or underfocusing on the problem usually causes an escalation of symptoms.

You know that something isn't quite right with your child. As your child gets older, she may not be keeping up with her classmates. The usual sorts of kids' problems are more severe and they aren't going away.

Outsiders say that something is wrong with your child. You may resent these comments, especially if they are meant to hurt rather than help. Your child probably hears these comments as well.

People imply that the difficulty is somehow your fault and that you should fix it. It doesn't take much for parents to wonder if the problem is related to something we should have done—or shouldn't have done.

You've had many referrals to counselors, social workers, pediatricians, psychologists, or psychiatrists. These referrals can be helpful, especially if you seek help relative to your concerns. Find a professional with whom you feel comfortable. If he or she won't return your calls or take time to explain things to you, find someone else.

You have ongoing struggles to know what to do or expect. You may alternate between wanting to protect your child from her problems and from other people, to pushing her to shape up. The constant thought through all of the struggles is, "I would do anything if someone would just tell me how to fix things."

You feel that nothing seems to work. Everything you have tried hasn't worked. Parenting techniques that work for other children simply don't work for your child.

Repeated Responses in Parenting the Special Needs Child

When parents aren't sure what to expect or what to do, it's easy to get stuck in these repeated responses.

Deny there is a problem. This may take the form of blaming circumstances, ignoring the most obvious symptoms, or refusing to talk about it. Your child may be quite different from your dream image of her. Her mental or physical difficulties may prevent her from doing the things you hoped for (star athlete, ballerina, teacher, chemist). Dealing with loss of the dream requires some grieving.

Focus on the difficulty, attempting to eliminate it. Getting rid of the problem would certainly be a positive outcome! Unfortunately, some problems can only be ameliorated. No one likes that option. Because parents want things fixed, they often shop for a doctor or a counselor who will provide the sure cure and completely eliminate the problem.

Blame self or others.

"If only the teacher hadn't said that . . ."
"If the doctor had suspected . . ."
"Why didn't I see that coming?"
"If his father hadn't . . ."

These are ways of attempting to deal with a frustrating situation. Unfortunately, assigning blame doesn't move you toward a solution.

Assigning blame doesn't move you toward a solution.

Overprotect your child. By now the child has been buffeted about by other children, adults, teachers, doctors, counselors, and a variety of psychological and medical treatments. It is natural that a parent would want to protect her from it all.

Underexpect from your child. Because you want to protect her, it is easy to overlook the strengths and positive attributes your child possesses, rather than allowing her to struggle with the problems. Not encouraging her to use those strengths may cause them to atrophy, or at least not to develop as they ought.

Put out fires. You always respond in a crisis mode to the current problem rather than operating on a well thought out, consistent plan. Obviously when there are crises, you must deal with them. Without a plan, however, the crises will continue to occur because you aren't changing what is causing them. (Even with a plan you won't be able to avert all crises.)

Give up and hand complete responsibility to others. You may hand the whole mess to your spouse, counselors, teachers, or the child. When this occurs, your valuable input is lost.

Did any of this sound familiar? Think about the factors that may keep you locked into one of these responses.

- Consider your beliefs. Your beliefs about how much control your child has over her symptoms will greatly influence how you interact with her. (See the chart on the following page.)

  The problem occurs when the child has some control but you aren't sure how much, and under what circumstances. And this may vary over time as well. Some adolescents who are down or bummed out can control their lives or emotions to a point and they can help themselves feel better. Some depressions are biological in nature and it is almost impossible to turn things around without an antidepressant medication. In the bummed out type of depression expecting them to pull themselves up by their bootstraps has some merit. But when in a biological depression, they may be incapable of doing the bootstraps number. Children with an ADD diagnosis aren't able to maintain their concentration for long periods of time no matter how much willpower they muster. The medication provides the needed assistance. Understanding and assessing how much control your child actually has is part of developing a new response.

Parent's Belief	Parent's Action	Reinforcement
1. Child has NO CONTROL over her behavior or problem. (No bowel or bladder control at 3 months of age.)	You must take charge and do it for her. (You buy diapers and change them as needed.)	Reinforcement and consequences are irrelevant. She has no control, so imposing consequences would be cruel.
2. Child has SOME CONTROL over her behavior or problem. (Sugar level in blood: She can't eliminate her diabetes but she can control what she eats, which affects her sugar level.)	You allow her to do what she can do and you pick up the slack. (You provide training, proper food, insulin, medical equipment.)	She should be expected to do what she can do. Consequences, rewards, and reinforcement are relevant. You then need to help with what she cannot do.
3. Child has COMPLETE CONTROL over her behavior or problem. (Flunking two classes simply because she has twelve missing assignments.)	You expect her to take charge of her behavior. (You limit her social activity until her grades improve.)	Your job is to teach, encourage, and expect her to control her behavior. You reinforce and provide relevant consequences when appropriate.

- Understand your underlying motivation. Positive parental motivation is not always helpful for the child. Parents are often driven by the following understandable motives.

  They want to fix the problem. Parents would like to eliminate the problem so their child could have the opportunity to be more like other children. But the problem may be one that can't be fixed. Both child and parents may need to spend energy adapting to the problem, rather than trying to fix it.

They want to protect their child. Parents would rather deal with the problem themselves than have their child continue to struggle. Any parent who hasn't thought that, and acted on that thought, probably doesn't care about his or her child. But she needs more than just your protection.

They want to avoid feeling guilty or blamed for the difficulty. If parents do feel guilty, they're more likely to overprotect and overdo for their child, thus interfering with her adaptation.

They want to have a normal family life. This is certainly a reasonable desire. They are simply tired of the continual strain.

- Examine your parents' example. Your parents may not have had to deal with anything similar to your situation, thus leaving you without an example to follow. But when there were tough situations did they pull together, blame, or leave? Their general response may still be a pattern you might be using. Was it an effective way of coping?
- Study your role(s). Does your role facilitate your child's ability to adapt or cope, or does it promote her passive acceptance?

Protector. Certainly one of our parental responsibilities is to provide protection, but if this role becomes too strong, it can interfere with the child's positive adjustment.

Quality Controller. This role balances the Protector. A single parent who is a Protector will often find a spouse who will expect a certain level of performance regardless of the problems. When these two roles are blended they work well. If they compete, clear expectations aren't presented to the child and a tremendous amount of turmoil is generated in the marriage.

Martyr. The Martyr has a ready-made situation if there is someone who needs help. He or she will do whatever needs to be done to help the child, even if it isn't good for the child.

- Check your relationships. In families who have a special needs child, it is easy to take sides. One parent usually assumes the primary care responsibilities for that child, while the other parent focuses on the other children. The primary-care parent knows the special needs child better and can easily advocate for her, which may include pushing other family members to be more sensitive to her needs. If those needs aren't satisfactorily considered, that parent can become resentful and even more protective. Of course the same may occur with the other parent, who can become resentful of the use of emotional and financial resources for one child to the detriment of the rest of the family. Parents, make sure you talk about those resentments and work them out so you continue to work together.

Step 2: Clarify Responsibility

Present Expectations

Parents in this situation have a difficult time knowing what rules to present to their child, and if they disagree on their child's abilities, it further complicates the issues. They want to hold her accountable, but aren't sure what to realistically expect. Because of the confusion, it is easy to deal with things on the spot, and not worry about the overall picture or plan.

If things are handled on a moment by moment basis, the child does not know what is actually expected of him or her–an undesirable state of affairs.

Monitor Compliance

Parents spend considerable time monitoring their child's behavior, hoping to find clues that will clarify the child's true potential. This can be extremely frustrating because the clue that clears everything up is rarely found. Unfortunately, monitoring their child's behavior and comparing it to the stated expectation or rule takes a second fiddle position. Focusing solely on finding the clue keeps the situation stuck, because the child doesn't learn the connection between cause and effect.

Enforce Consequences

Not knowing what the child can actually do makes enforcement an unclear task. If the child truly doesn't understand the expectations or simply is incapable of achieving the expected behavior, punishing her would be cruel. On the other hand, if she does know the expectations and can do the behavior, but chooses to disobey, she should be disciplined.

Generally, parents err on the side of expecting too little. An error on this side means they do more work and the child does less. If they err on the side of expecting too much, they set the child up to fail and then punish her for something she is incapable of doing. This would be vicious and inhumane.

Step 3: Make a Plan to Change Your Response

Determine the Goal

The goal is to help the child minimize the negative effects of her particular difficulty, and to lead a productive life. She must learn to cope with and compensate for her problem.

As realistically as possible, the monkey should be gradually transferred to her back. When you have a reasonable handle on what your child is capable of, you can begin to encourage her to assume responsibility for those areas in her life. You can then change your response to a recycled response as indicated below. When you change you will be assisting her to change.

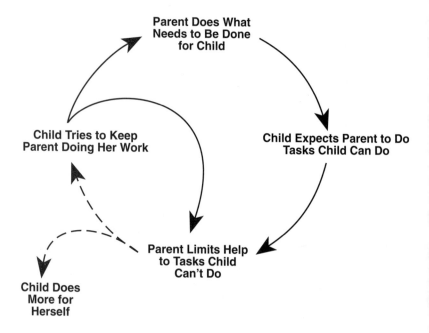

Develop a Plan

Get Child a Complete Medical Exam

Have a complete medical examination done by a qualified physician to identify or rule out physical causes. If there are physical causes for the problems or the behavior, counseling and the use of reinforcements and consequences will have minimal effect. Over the years I have counseled with a number of families who primarily needed medical treatment. Of course we didn't know that at first. But after checking physical components, we found such things as juvenile diabetes, brain anomalies, extreme premenstrual syndrome, allergies, malfunctioning thyroid, ADD, and mental illnesses such as schizophrenia, bipolar disorder, depression. All of these either have a physical basis or a physically appropriate treatment. If there is suspected drug or alcohol use, a drug screen and appropriate drug treatment would be in order. Trying to counsel the child, adolescent, or adult to behave differently would have had little effect prior to the medical treatment. However, counseling may become a secondary part of the overall treatment approach.

Follow Through on Recommendations

Recommendations may include such services as inpatient treatment, medication, psychological testing, in-home services, family counseling, group counseling, individual counseling, support groups, educational reading material. Be sure you understand why these recommendations are being made and what you must do to follow through on them.

If medication is prescribed, your child should take it as directed. Generally with ADD and antidepressant medications, there is a trial stage. During this time the medications are given in smaller doses to test their effect. Certain antidepressants work better for some people than for others, so finding a good match requires a little patience. The right dosage of medication for ADD is usually fine tuned by starting at a low level and then increasing it to reach the therapeutic dosage. Be sure to ask about side effects associated with whatever medication is prescribed.

Gather Information

Gather as much information as possible and then use it to develop clear guidelines and procedures for dealing with your child.

What exactly is the problem? Be very specific. Sometimes it is useful to define the problem in behavioral terms. For example, "Jenny has a bad attitude" doesn't help much. "She doesn't take out the garbage on time" gives more useful information.

When is it a problem? Mark a calendar to see when it occurs, and see if there is a pattern or a logical reason why it occurs at those points. One child I worked with always seemed to have trouble on Mondays. We came to realize that he never got enough sleep on Sunday nights because Dad, in his desire to spend as much time as possible with the child, was always late returning him to Mom's house. That was helpful information in figuring out a treatment plan.

Where is it a problem? If it only occurs at school and not at home, you may want to schedule a meeting with teachers and administrators to get their input. What differences at school may aggravate the problem?

How often is it a problem? Monitor the frequency. It may not be as big a problem as you thought. This information will also be useful when the child begins to make progress. If your children fight thirty times a week, only fifteen would be progress!

For whom is it a problem? This question deals with monkey ownership. If the problem only bothers you, your child will have no motivation to make the situation better. If that is the case, you may want to consider if you are overreacting or what you can do so it isn't such a problem for you.

If you're the only one actively trying to improve something that legitimately needs to be changed, ask yourself, "What could I do to motivate others to help improve this?"

What are the events surrounding the problem? Sometimes the events can give clues to the general theme of the problem. Is your child only flunking classes with female teachers? If this occurs, you may have a pattern of difficulty with females. You may further discover that she has a problem with a specific female that is being generalized to all women.

When is the problem better? When is it not as much of a problem? This may give you clues as to what seems to work. If you can find something specific that seems to make things better, is there a way you can do more of that?

How do others contribute? When the problem happens, what specifically do family members do? Does it make sense for them to continue doing that? How well does it work? What other things could they do? Have a brainstorming session to see if there are other alternatives that no one has suggested. One family fought over housecleaning–everyone hated doing it! Because all family members worked, they decided to chip in and have a cleaning lady come twice a month.

What support does your child have or need? If she identifies specifics that would be helpful and you can provide them, provide that support. If she says that she wants nothing, that may be what you have to provide for a while. This will either cause things to get worse or will challenge her to succeed. If things get worse, she will gain a more accurate picture of her situation. If she discovers that she can handle the situation fine, she has built her self-esteem.

What support do other family members need? To positively deal with the problem, do parents or siblings need counseling, extra attention and reassurance, special activities or times for themselves?

Establish a Clear Structure

Certain difficulties, such as ADD, or a brain defect or injury, make it very hard to know what to expect from your child. In such cases, the external structure is even more crucial. If she truly doesn't understand, the structure will help her learn the connection between behavior and consequence. If she does understand, the structure will reinforce her when making the right decision. When it is difficult to determine how much control the child has over her symptoms, focus your energy on developing a clear structure. Parental unity and commitment to the structure are crucial, or the child receives two different messages about how to behave. To eliminate this confusion, parents need to

Develop crystal clear expectations and consequences. Start with small expectations and reinforce what you know she can do. Take time to be pleased with what she is doing. For new behaviors, explain what you want, and reinforce the direction you wish to see your child take. This process is known as *shaping.* For example, you want Lisa to clean up her room. By the use of shaping, you would reinforce any type of picking-up behavior. You can do that on a very small basis and begin to reinforce behavioral changes. If you wait to say anything positive until she has cleaned her entire room, you may be waiting for a long time. Initially, positive and negative consequences need to be as immediate as possible to establish the link between behavior and consequence.

Establish a daily schedule with activities and time slots. This is particularly important with young children who have focusing and attention problems. If your child doesn't have the internal cognitive skills to organize herself, then an external schedule is needed to provide the appropriate amount of organization. When you have established a working schedule, do your best to stick with it. After following a schedule for a while, our bodies adapt to it, so let that work for you. A bedtime routine helps children prepare for sleep. By the time the routine is completed, the child's body knows it is time to sleep.

Teach the specific things you would like to see your child do. Identify and teach developmentally appropriate skills. Some of those will need to be modified as time progresses, but the goal is to help the child do as much for herself as possible, whenever possible.

Practice

Use the following chart to practice your new responses and limit your old ones.

Parental Behaviors

Date to evaluate: _____

Practice New Response	SUN	MON	TUES	WED	THU	FRI	SAT
Limited my help to those things she couldn't do herself							
Followed through on appropriate encouragement and consequences, positive and negative							
Taught appropriate skills and encouraged practice							
Posted and stuck with a daily schedule (or a schedule for the things that cause difficulty)							
Supported child to deal with her emotions regarding her needs and differences							

Limit Old Response	SUN	MON	TUES	WED	THU	FRI	SAT
Felt sorry for child and didn't allow her to really work at managing her problem							
Did for her things she could do for herself							
Did all of the adjusting or accommodating							
Excused her behavior because of her special problems							

Put an *X* in the corresponding days where the behavior was present. The *X*s are desirable in the top chart and undesirable in the bottom one.

Anticipate Your Child's Reaction

When you increase your expectations and limit your protectiveness, your child may do any of the following.

Deny there is a problem. You may hear statements like: "Everything is fine." "I don't think I have a problem." "Will you stop bugging me? Everything is under control." In spite of her reassurances, things aren't okay, and she hasn't handled her problem. You probably can't talk her into admitting that she has a problem, so let circumstances and your clear structure help her see that she needs to change her approach to the problem.

Be angry that you stopped doing things for her. She may be angry directly or indirectly, verbally or behaviorally. From a younger child you may hear: "Why did you stop doing that for me? You know I can't do that. I hate you!" From an older child you may hear: "That's fine. If you aren't going to do it, it just won't get done. See if I care."

Stage a slowdown strike or regress in what she is willing to do for herself. The child will attempt to modify your behavior by changing her behavior. If you want more (put away her clothes), she will give you less (stop dressing herself) until you stop wanting more. When you stop expecting more, she may return to doing what she was doing (dressing herself but not putting away her clothes).

Resist the prescribed medication. Your child may resist the medication by passively "forgetting" it or actively refusing to take it. If you are getting a significant amount of resistance, the child may not clearly understand the purpose and meaning of the medication. Most of the time the child has received an adequate explanation of the medication's purpose either from the physician or the parent. Problems often occur, however, concerning the meaning of the medication. The child needs to deal with why she must take the medication. She may feel she is defective. The presentation concerning the medication obviously can make a difference.

> **Presentation 1:** "Taking the medication will make you a good girl." (Conversely, not taking the medication makes her a bad girl. How excited would you be to take the medicine if it was the only way to be a good girl? The medication gets the credit for the positive changes, and she gets the credit for the bad things.)

> **Presentation 2:** "The medicine will make it easier for you to concentrate, so you can do better in school."

Avoid tying the medication to her self-esteem. Instead, focus on the function of the medication.

Threaten to run away to someone who will "take better care" of her. She may want to be with Grandma or someone who will give her what she wants. Don't allow this threat to trigger your guilt, diverting your efforts to help her cope with her needs.

Be aware of the old cues that cause you to overprotect. Don't let them hinder you from supporting your child's growth. And remember, she will not like talking about the problem and will try to avoid anything related to it. Once she sees that you are firm in wanting her to be actively involved and you are firm in your support, she will begin to try new ways of behaving.

Set a Date to Review the Plan

Make sure you evaluate the plan on the date scheduled. A point of accountability helps us all stay focused on the issues.

Step 4: Evaluate and Modify the Plan

Evaluate the Plan

Direction

Being clear with appropriate expectations and allowing your child to struggle a bit more than usual will likely cause you to feel guilty for not fixing it for her. But if you see her assuming more control over her life, and feeling good about the things she can do, you know you are heading in the right direction! If you are backing off the amount of control you assert over a situation, and your child is picking up some of that control, you are making progress!

Expectations

Before considering how far you are from your goal, take time to look at what you did to make progress this week.

Evaluate Your Behavior and Feelings

1. Did you feel good about your behavior?
2. With which specific goals did you succeed?
3. What did you do to make that progress?
4. Has that changed your level of anger or frustration?
5. What was hard for you?
6. What did your spouse do well?
7. Did you tell him or her?

Evaluate Your Child's Behavior and Feelings

1. Did your plan have any effect on your child?
2. Did your plan appropriately place more of your child's responsibility back on her shoulders?

Review the chart you made and see what you did well. What worked, and is there a way to do more of that?

Modify the Plan

Using the answers in the preceding section, what can you do to make the plan work better? If both you and your spouse agree on the changes, it is likely that they are good changes.

Commit to the Revised Plan

Commit to the new plan and set a date to see how it worked. Try the changes for a week and see!

Parents must not become too focused on the limitations or on the diagnosis.

Erik Erikson's "Eight Stages of Man" describes developmental conflicts that occur in the human life cycle.* At ages six to twelve the main question your child is trying to answer is *What can I do?* The question your adolescent is trying to answer is *Who am I?* To help the special needs child or adolescent answer these questions, parents must not become too focused on the limitations or on the diagnosis. Here is a summary of what we must do.

> *Protect, but don't overprotect.* Overprotecting would tell the child that she can't do much, and that she is forever a victim of her problem.
> *Accept the diagnosis, but don't allow it to become the child's identity.* Identifying her as the diagnosis would limit her adaptive behavior and tell her that she is nothing more than the diagnosis ("This is Sarah, my diabetic.").

*E. H. Erikson, *Childhood and Society,* 2nd ed. (New York: Norton, 1963).

Monitor the symptoms but neither scrutinize nor ignore them. Monitoring the symptoms tells your daughter that with your help she can learn to deal with her symptoms, and that you value her above her problems.

Cope, don't surrender or deny. Coping with her problems tells her that she has valuable strength, and that she can use her strength to be the best she can be. She can be a survivor rather than a victim.

The following comparisons briefly outline certain behaviors along a continuum:

Protect	**versus**	**Overprotect**
Parent		*Parent*
1. Understand the difficulty		1. Say no to everything based on fear
2. Seek and obtain appropriate care (medical, counseling, training)		2. Do for child what he can do for himself
3. Set reasonable safety standards		3. Revolve entire life around difficulty
4. Know warning signs		
5. Develop plan for emergencies		
Child		*Child*
1. Say no to activities that trigger reactions or problems		1. Never try anything new
2. Keep healthy (eat, exercise, and sleep properly)		2. Fiercely rebel against over-protection

Accept	**versus**	**Identify**
Parent		*Parent*
1. Come to grips with what the problem means about your child		1. Think of child as primarily diabetic, epileptic, etc.
2. Come to grips with what the problem means about you as a parent		2. Always use "asthmatic" or "hyper" when speaking of her
3. Attend support group (if available), or find other parents with similar difficulties to gain insight and practical information		3. Focus your attention exclusively on asthma, ADD, seizures, blood sugar level, etc.
		4. Miss child's positive behavior

Accept	versus	Identify
Child		*Child*

Child (Accept):
1. Come to grips with what it means to have this difficulty
2. Face and accept need for medication
3. Understand limitations

Child (Identify):
1. Focus on limitations
2. Use difficulty as reason to do nothing, get attention, or gain sympathy

Monitor Symptoms	versus	Scrutinize or Ignore

Parent (Monitor Symptoms):
1. Notice important symptoms
2. Know progression of symptoms
3. Provide medication when needed
4. Help child to become more aware, more responsible

Parent (Scrutinize or Ignore):
1. Be hypervigilant regarding symptoms
2. Overrespond to symptoms
3. Ignore obvious symptoms

Child (Monitor Symptoms):
1. Understand symptoms
2. Be alert to symptoms
3. Ask for medication when needed

Child (Scrutinize or Ignore):
1. Deny or ignore symptoms
2. Refuse to take medication
3. Want extra medication

Cope	versus	Surrender or Deny

Parent (Cope):
1. Observe child's total behavior (not just symptoms or difficulties)
2. Spend positive time with child
3. Develop realistic expectations (revise frequently)
4. Deal with own feelings
5. Discuss the problems
6. Reinforce alternate strengths, activities
7. Encourage good judgment
8. Clarify responsibility (Who should have the monkey?)

Parent (Surrender or Deny):
1. Expect too much or too little
2. Don't go to counseling
3. Don't talk about the problem
4. Don't advise appropriate people of child's limitations or concerns

(continued)

(continued from page 193)

Cope	versus	Surrender or Deny
Child		*Child*
1. Deal with own feelings		1. Give up
2. Cooperate with medical care		2. Don't acknowledge abilities or
3. Develop strengths		limitations
4. Develop other interests		
5. Ask for or earn positive attention		

Staying on the positive side can be a challenge as things change from day to day. Take heart; you don't have to be perfect parents. Being aware of the issues, supporting each other, and trusting God to assist you will help keep the balance (see Philippians 1:6).

12

We're Walking on Eggshells

Rut 7: Emotional Blackmail

Threats work. They can evoke great fear in parents, causing them to give in or to not cross the child.

> Now Adonijah the son of Haggith exalted himself, saying, "I will be king." So he prepared for himself chariots and horsemen with fifty men to run before him. And his father had never crossed him at any time by asking, "Why have you done so?"
>
> 1 Kings 1:5–6

David never crossed Adonijah. We aren't specifically told the reason for Dad's behavior, but it certainly is consistent with a parent who is afraid to voice an opinion for fear of how the child will respond. If you are a parent who walks on eggshells, you know how strongly children can react.

Boys are likely to use verbal and physical intimidation. If your son doesn't like your answer, he may get in your face and call you foul names. If that doesn't work, he may escalate to shoving, hitting, or other abusive behavior. He will push until you're scared enough to give him what he wants.

Girls may use intimidation, but are more likely to use the threat of never speaking to you, never forgiving you, doing drugs, getting pregnant, running away, or committing suicide. Some of these threats, of course, are every bit as frightening to caring parents as physical intimidation.

Claiming child abuse is the other biggie a child may use to get his way. If parents attempt to control the child by physical means (restraint or spanking), or not doing what the child wants, he threatens to report them to Social Services. Parents who have been reported for child abuse, regardless of what the outcome was, often feel that all of their parental power has been stripped away. What little control they previously had is gone.

Step 1: Recognize Emotional Blackmail

Is This the Picture in Your Home?

In this rut, the child gets what he wants primarily through the use of threats and the behavior associated with those threats. If this rut occurs in your family, you probably see the following.

A child is out of control. He demands or does what he wants, paying no attention to parental directives or concerns.

Parents are afraid and worried. They see they are in a bad situation that could result in physical harm to themselves or their child. His behavior is becoming more serious and he ignores all consequences.

The child's threatening behavior is escalating. Because he wants more and more, the threats increase in number and seriousness.

The child experiences an increasing number of conflicts with authority figures outside of the home. Because the threats work at home, he tries them in other settings. But people outside of the home don't always respond to threats by giving in. This creates serious problems for him.

The child is completely uninterested in counseling, talking, or changing his behavior. He views any change in the status quo only as a way of losing power. Why should he go to counseling when he will lose his main tool for getting what he wants? His response usually is, "You can't make me go to counseling." Sometimes he is less defiant and says, "I will go, but you can't make me talk."

A crisis is developing. The child may push things to the point where you absolutely must draw a line. Can you continue to let him be gone all night with the car when you know he is drinking and has no driver's license?

Repeated Responses in Emotional Blackmail

It is easy for parents to get stuck in these repeated responses.

Give in to the threats to avoid blowups. Parents hope that by giving in the immediate crisis will be avoided and things will settle down. Usually the immediate crisis is averted, but the problem doesn't end. The child continues to push for more and more of what he wants. Naturally he will continue to use this strategy as long as his parents give in.

Let issues slide. By not making an issue out of some topics, parents hope their child will be more cooperative. However, the child may view this as permission to do what he wishes, or as surrender to his superior power.

Minimize or rationalize their feelings and concerns. Parents often minimize the importance of their feelings. Their discontent is clearly easier to cope with than his angry outbursts. So the parents make the adjustment and give the child what he wants. A parent might say, "It really wasn't that big a deal.

Yes, he hit me, but it didn't hurt that much. He was just so upset because he couldn't go see his girlfriend."

This parent has thus talked himself or herself out of doing anything about the physical confrontation.

Blame others—spouse, relatives—for the problems. Spouses frequently get blamed for the child's behavior. In the past, one parent may have done something that didn't have the blessing of the other parent. That decision now is the key issue preventing parental agreement. Of course, it is much easier to blame and to focus on the previous problem because it has less volatility than the current battle with the child.

Limit responses to those that won't upset the child (walking on eggshells). Because parents narrow their range of responses, over time they forget, or don't realize, their combined strength to deal with adversity and difficulties. They may also overlook resources available for them through their church, family, or community.

Use physical force to regain control of the situation. Sometimes this can be helpful, and other times it can be very negative. If you have a six year old who is out of control and is telling you he is going to leave, physically restraining him until he becomes more reasonable is quite appropriate. If you have a fifteen-year-old who is headed for the door with a full head of steam, trying to stop him physically may result in someone getting hurt. Usually an alternate plan is a better option, which you and your spouse need to have previously established.

Did any of this sound familiar? Think about the factors that may keep you locked into one of these responses.

- Consider your beliefs. There are two major parental beliefs that fuel this pattern. You believe that your child might actually follow through on his threats, and that you are impotent to do anything about it.

Parents who believe both of these must continue to give in. In order to change the pattern you must realize that these beliefs can be dealt with separately. Unfortunately, nothing is going to change the first belief. Your child may follow through on what he threatens to do. That's his decision, and is out of your control. However, the second belief can be changed. You can decide how to deal with the situation. Are you going to continue your reactions because of the threats? If you decide to stop giving in to the threats, you will want to determine the time and place to stop. Specifics for formulating a plan will be discussed later in the chapter.

- Understand your underlying motivation. Parental motivation is usually understandable. Most parents give in because they want to avoid

     A blowup
     Making things worse than they already are
     Feeling guilty for what might occur
     Fear and embarrassment resulting from child's behavior
     Difficult decisions or uncomfortable situations
     A major tragedy–pregnancy, runaway, homicide, suicide

- Examine your parents' example. Your parents may have set the example that might makes right. If this occurred, you may have unknowingly adopted that rule in your family. This means as kids get older, and bigger, they may assert their prerogative to be right by having the most might. Remember how they do what we do?

In some families, women marry men who rule by physical force or verbal intimidation. If this occurred in your family, you learned that it is okay for men to rule in this manner and women should tolerate it. A woman in this situation is less likely to give her parental input, and the man is less likely to accept it. This dynamic can also give permission to the boys in the family to demean and abuse Mom or their sisters.

- Study your role(s). Several roles may be operative in this pattern:

     Caspar Milquetoast. In this role the parent doesn't exert any power, creating a vacuum for the child to fill with his power.
     Victim. A parent in this role is waiting for someone to take advantage of him or her. This makes it very easy for the child to take over, telling the parent what he is going to do and how the parent is to respond.

- Check your relationships. It may be that your child gets the power to rule from an alliance with your spouse. Parents will have great difficulty curtailing the threats if they aren't in agreement about proper behavior. Where is the child obtaining his power?

Step 2: Clarify Responsibility

Present Expectations

Parents in this pattern usually don't present the rules, and if they do speak up, it is in general statement with only a suggestive tone. This is a natural approach if you are worried about upsetting your child or causing him to be angry. To correct this situation, the parents need to be clear and specific in what they expect. When this is done, the child certainly won't like it. This will undoubtedly create a crisis, so a comprehensive plan needs to be in place prior to enforcing consequences.

Monitor Compliance

Parents monitor their child's behavior with great sensitivity. They monitor him, however, not to hold him accountable for his disobedience, but to know whether he is apt to explode.

Enforce Consequences

Parents don't enforce the rules they expect their child to follow. Instead, they are focused on preventing blowups and keeping things safe. Their perceived loss of power and their fear keep them from following through on consequences.

Step 3: Make a Plan to Change Your Response

Determine the Goal

The goal is to remove the power from the child's threats, and restore parental power to make appropriate decisions

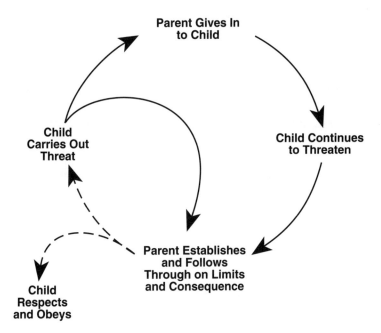

regarding the child. Your change in behavior will assist him to change.

Develop a Plan

Assess the Situation

Identify your fears. What specifically are they? These often include the fear of physical harm or death to the parent or the child, loss of contact, an undesirable event—flunking a grade, doing drugs, getting pregnant.

Are the fears realistic? Do you have good reason to believe that your child would follow through on his threats? If there is a history of the negative behavior, the chances are higher that he might follow through. And if he has a plan, he is more apt to do it, particularly if he has the means available to him (guns, pills, car). Alcohol and drug usage also increase the probability that he would do something drastic.

Identify your strengths and your ability to deal with the situation. What strengths and resources can you use to deal more effectively with your child? Are you working cooperatively with your spouse?

If you are to overcome your child's power and threats, you must work together. If you can't, it will be much harder to turn things around. In most cases, a young child who is completely out of control has obtained some of his power from an adult in his life. Look to see where he may be getting his power—a lenient or weak spouse? Grandparents who spoil him excessively? If possible, talk to that person and see if he or she would give the child a clear message regarding appropriate behavior. Cut off the power leak!

What options are available in your church or community for preventing your fear from becoming a reality, or for dealing with it if it does occur?

Make Planned, Conscious Decisions

Decide if things will get better or worse if left alone. At this point, you have reached a fork in the road. You must decide on one route. Unfortunately you cannot take both roads and have things change.

One road is labeled Draw a Line in the Sand. This tells the child that you won't tolerate a specific behavior any longer and that you are prepared to do what it takes to back up your expectations. The other road is labeled Hope and Pray He Self-Corrects.

Vacillating between the two simply will not work. If you choose to back off, you must allow the natural consequences to occur. Clearly the age of the child will significantly impact which road you choose. An eight year old cannot be allowed to threaten and get away with it. A seventeen year old may be tolerated long enough until he leaves the home. If you choose to draw the line in the sand, you need to be together and committed to following that course of action.

Determine the point at which you will no longer respond to his threats. By choosing time, place, and issue, you can address safety concerns. If safety is a major issue (homicide, suicide), make sure you have needed services in place before making your move. Remove all pills, guns, knives, and other lethal weapons from his access.

Determine with your spouse how you will respond to each escalation of your child's behavior. What will you do if he

Cusses you out?
Punches a hole in the wall?
Pushes or punches you? Your spouse?
Leaves the house without permission?
Leaves in the car without permission, and perhaps without a license?

Who could you call for assistance? Those who usually help include your spouse, relatives, friends, pastor, counselor, the police. Have the necessary people prepared so the situation doesn't get out of control.

Are you willing to hospitalize him for his protection, particularly if suicidal? Find out what your insurance covers. Does your insurance cover mental health problems?

The important thing is to be clear and firm. Trying to intimidate or threaten him is inappropriate. You must simply let him know that you are prepared to do what needs to be done. When he sees that you mean business and aren't going to back down, he may cooperate. He may also attempt to follow through on his threats. Think about each of these issues so you have a plan you feel comfortable with if he decides to push things to the extreme. Be prepared.

Have a Safety Net in Place

Make sure you have a safety net in place before implementing your plan. Having the child take a time-out with a relative or friend, or having him placed at a hospital or juvenile facility may be helpful in reducing the immediate danger. Parents should decide if that is necessary, who he will stay with, for how long, and under what conditions he may return home. Most communities have places for juveniles to stay for brief time-outs. If that is your plan, make sure they have an opening before implementing your plan!

Lead Your Family to Healthier Ways

Learn to resolve differences in healthier and safer ways. The child needs support to deal with the expectations. You need support to remain strong and clear.

Attend a Tough Love group or other support groups
Arrange for a counselor to see your child and your family
Obtain a Big Brother or Big Sister for your child
Discuss it with your pastor and have him talk with your child

Write down the goals you have for your family and specify steps to reach those goals.

Parental Behaviors

Date to evaluate: _____

Practice New Response	SUN	MON	TUES	WED	THU	FRI	SAT
Committed to parental unity and dealt with situations together							
Made specific plan to deal with escalating behavior							
Clearly laid out expectations and consequences for the child							
Followed through on appropriate consequences, positive and negative							
Used parental power appropriately for good of child and family							

Limit Old Response	SUN	MON	TUES	WED	THU	FRI	SAT
Gave in to avoid blowups; made decisions based on fear							
Avoided issues; walked on eggshells							
Blamed spouse or others for child's unacceptable behavior							
Took a passive role							

Practice

Use the chart on the previous page to practice your new responses and limit your old ones. Put an *X* in the corresponding days where the behavior was present. The *X*s are desirable in the top chart and undesirable in the bottom one.

Anticipate Your Child's Reaction

Because your child routinely uses power as a way of getting what he wants, he won't change without a struggle. You will likely see him do the following.

Ignore your demands and do what he wants to do. He really doesn't expect that you will change anything. You have given in previously, and there is no reason to assume that you will do anything differently now. Thus he simply ignores your demands, assuming nothing will come of them. Even though he is ignoring the demands, don't assume that he is ignoring you, however. He probably is paying close attention to what you are doing. Will you follow through? Will you drop your demands? Will you be too scared to impose the consequences?

Your child will continue to make power plays to get what he wants.

Increase his threats. Typically, the child responds to your firmness with an increase in the frequency or the seriousness of his threats. If you won't back down to his runaway threat, perhaps you will to a suicide threat. The conversation may go something like this one between Angie and her mother.

"If you don't let me go to the dance on Friday night, I won't come home Friday after school. I *am* going to the dance."

"Your father and I agreed that you lost your weekend privileges for this week because you didn't make your curfew last week. You know that is the rule."

"Then I just won't come home after school on Friday. You can't stop me from going to the dance."

"You don't have our permission to go."

"If you try to stop me from going, you'll be sorry 'cuz I'll just kill myself."

If her mother gives in at this point, Angie learns that suicidal threats work! Can you guess what she will use the next time she really wants something?

If you accept the monkey, the rut won't change.

Follow through on part or all of his threat. At a certain point, your teen may feel like he must follow through on his threats—you can only threaten so long until you have to come through. He may have painted himself into a corner, or has a high need to save face. If he does carry out his threat, it is quite likely that he will blame his behavior on you.

"I wouldn't have had to hit you if you hadn't kept saying I couldn't go. If you would just let me go, I wouldn't have to get so violent."

If you accept the monkey, the rut won't change.

Don't forget that the cues that prompt you to give in—threatening, gestures, violence—are still lurking. When you start to change, he will increase his threatening, or actually carry out one of the threats he has made. That is why it is important to have a comprehensive plan in place so you can deal with each of his possible responses. When he sees that the threats will no longer work, he will begin to develop other ways of meeting his needs.

Set a Date to Review the Plan

Set a date to review the plan in about a week. This should give you ample time to try the plan and to determine its viability.

207

Step 4: Evaluate and Modify the Plan

Evaluate the Plan

Direction

If you are clear and firm in your directives, and are not making decisions based solely on your fear, you are facing the right direction! Remember, God has not given us the spirit of fear (2 Tim. 1:6).

Expectations

Take time to review what went well, so you can do more of that. Review the chart to feel good about your progress.

Evaluate Your Behavior and Feelings

1. Did you feel good about your behavior?
2. With which specific goals did you succeed?
3. What did you do to make that progress?
4. Has that changed your level of anger or frustration?
5. What was hard for you?
6. What did your spouse do well?
7. Did you tell him or her?

Evaluate Your Child's Behavior and Feelings

1. Did your plan have any effect on your child?
2. Did your plan appropriately place more of your child's responsibility back on his shoulders?

Modify the Plan

After looking at what seemed to work, figure out a way to do more of that. In reviewing the chart you may find that it was very difficult to follow through on your plan when tension escalated. Use this information to change either the plan or the consequence.

Commit to the Revised Plan

Try the new plan for a week and see how it works. Be sure to let at least one other person know what you are doing so he or she can encourage you and pray for you.

In this emotional blackmail pattern, parents must carefully weigh the situation, move beyond their ambivalence, and firmly commit themselves to a course of action. If they wish to change, they must be prepared and willing to take whatever actions are necessary to show their child that they will respond to each and every threat. Remaining firm to the first three threats and then giving in to the fourth one actually escalates the situation.

Say yes as much as you can, and when you say no be prepared to do what needs to be done to stick with it!

13

The Impassable Rut

Overcoming

As newlyweds, Bonnie and I often went to the ranch for a break from college life. On this particular visit it was cold and snowing, with the wind blowing fiercely. These storms are quite common in Wyoming and so is getting stuck! When we turned off the highway onto the dirt road lined on both sides by barbed wire, the visibility was poor and I could see that the last mile would be the hardest part of the journey. But I thought we could make it—I had been over this road many times and knew each bump and turn.

A frozen rut made following the road much easier. But as the rut grew deeper and deeper, we realized that the previous traveler had high-centered and gotten stuck. Not wanting to repeat his experience, I stopped our vehicle and walked ahead to investigate. The snow was very deep and the rut very hard. If we were to make it through, we would have to get a good run at it. As I shifted into four-wheel drive and backed up, I said, "Ready, Bonnie? Hang on!"

You guessed it—we didn't make it. By rocking back and forth I was able to back up about twenty feet, but now what could we do? There was no way to go forward through the drift—we would have to choose a new path.

As we considered our options, I remembered that the previous summer my father and I had fixed the barbed wire on the fence so it could be lowered—for just such a time as this. With the fence lowered, I hoped we could get out of the rut, travel through the ditch that ran next to the road, over the wire, and onto the prairie. Not being from Wyoming, Bonnie wasn't too excited about the ditch plan, but I assured her it would work, most likely. I paused to look ahead once more, and then at the ditch and the prairie beyond. It was time to commit. We opted for the prairie.

Earlier in the day, going to the ranch seemed like a good idea.

We tightened our seat belts, I revved the engine and took off. With some speed and a hard right, we popped out of the rut and headed for the ditch. For a brief moment, I wondered if the rut wasn't a better place! The ditch was rough, and deeper than I'd anticipated, but our forward momentum carried us through it to the open prairie. The good news was that we were out of the rut! The bad news was that the prairie wasn't as familiar as the road.

The challenge now was to watch carefully that we didn't drive into a gully filled level with snow. To avoid such traps, we watched for weeds sticking out of the snow. The places where we couldn't see weeds were likely to be much deeper. Funny thing about those weeds—they had been a nuisance during the summer, but now they were friends. Help sometimes comes in strange-looking packages!

At first we stopped about every ten feet to get out and look for weeds. But as we progressed, I became less concerned and didn't think I needed to stop to check my bearings. Five minutes later, thoroughly stuck in a huge drift, I had to admit we wouldn't make it without help.

I was glad I had called my parents to let them know what time to expect us. We hoped they were watching for us, would realize our dilemma, and would arrive momentarily. By the time I had dug out the front tires and was shoveling around the back ones, I saw a truck approaching. Sure enough, it was my father with chains on his truck and a load of hay for extra traction. He hitched a chain to our bumper and pulled us out of the drift. By following the new path he made, we reached the ranch house, where a fire in the fireplace and hot chocolate awaited us.

I had to admit
we wouldn't make it without help.

It was not an easy trip. The visibility was bad, the rut was impassable, the ditch was deep. The prairie was unfamiliar, the gullies were annoying, and the last drift was a stopper.

Rearing children is likewise difficult, and you can find yourselves stuck in an impassable rut. But with a change in direction, some teamwork, frequent checking of your bearings, and help from your Father, you too can complete the journey.

Richard L. Berry is assistant director for Youth Alternatives, Cheyenne, Wyoming, and conducts family therapy sessions, focusing on families with adolescents. He has previously worked with the district attorney's office in Greeley, Colorado, coordinating three juvenile diversion court programs, and served as director of the Midwestern Colorado Youth Center in Montrose, Colorado. A graduate of Denver Seminary, he also has a PsyD. in counseling psychology from the University of Northern Colorado. He and his wife, Bonnie, have three children.